Navigate Your Existence!

7 Keys to the African American Resurrection

Omiyale Jubé

Navigate Your Existence!
7 Keys to the African American Resurrection
By Omiyale Jubé

Copyright © 2012
By Omiyale Jubé

All rights reserved. No part of this work may be reproduced or transmitted in any form by any means, electronic or mechanical, including photocopying, recording, or any other informational retrieval system, without the permission of the publisher, except by a reviewer who may quote brief passages or reproduce illustrations in a review with the appropriate credits.

www.NavigateYourExistence.com

First edition

ISBN: 978-0-9897182-0-2

The information in this book is expressed as the author's opinion based on research and personal experiences. It is not intended to belittle anyone's religious beliefs or convictions regarding life. This information is not intended to be used as a medical diagnosis or prescription for any physical, emotional, or mental ailments. Anyone seeking medical advice should personally meet with a qualified health practitioner. In the event that you use any technique or practice in this book, do so at your own discretion, as the author and publisher assume no responsibility.

DEDICATION

*This book is dedicated to:
My Brothers and Sisters of
the African American Community,
the Africans across the Diaspora,
the Indigenous People of the World,
and
the Human Collective*

*A people with no knowledge of self
is like
a tree with no roots*

African Proverb

Table of Contents

List of Illustrations xi

Foreword xiii

Acknowledgements. xv

Preface – From the Pyramids to the Projects –
From the Projects to the Stars. xvii

Introduction – Conductor of the Ship 1

PART ONE: CHART THE COURSE 11
    Chart the Course – Introduction 13

RECOGNIZE The Anchors of Limitation

Chapter 1: *My Story: The Journey Begins*. 15
    The Journey Begins 15
    A Doorway to Higher Awareness 24

Chapter 2: *Anchors of Limitation* 31
    Identify Your Belief Systems. 32
    Analyze Your Anchors 33

    Freedom to Succeed *36*

    Catch the Wave – *Chapter Summary*. *38*

RESTORE The Knowledge of the Ancestors

Chapter 3: *Time Waits For No One* 43

    What Time Is It? 43

    2012 and Beyond. 44

    Astrology: Real or Fantasy?. 56

    The Age of Aquarius. 59

    Catch the Wave – *Chapter Summary*. *61*

Chapter 4: *Everything Is Connected* 65

    Is This Statue Solid?. 66

    Everything Is Made of the Same Stuff 72

    Eastside/Westside 73

    Catch the Wave – *Chapter Summary*. *84*

Chapter 5: *Now You See It - Now You Don't* 87

    Omniscient Forces. 88

    Seven Dimensions 92

    Transition to a Fifth Dimensional Planet 99

    The Times…They-Are-a-Changing 101

    Catch the Wave – *Chapter Summary*. *103*

Chapter 6: *New Age/Ancient Wisdom* 107

    The Universal Laws 108

    The Law Divine Oneness 110

    The Law of Vibration. 110

    The Law of Cause and Effect 112

    The Law of Attraction 113

RESPONSIBILITY – Take Responsibility

RELEASE – The Anchors

    A Shift Toward Taking Control 116

    Karma And Reincarnation 116

    A Long Look in the Mirror 120

    Universal Laws and Sub-Laws 123

    Catch the Wave – *Chapter Summary*. *128*

PART TWO: START THE ENGINES 133

    Start the Engines – Introduction 135

REACTIVATE – Your Energy Sources

Chapter 7: *Melanin, Energy, and You* 139

    Melanin: What Is It? 141

    Melanin: What Does It Do? 142

    Melanin, Race, and the Color Issue 144

    The Disconnect 150

    Reactivate Your Melanin 155

    Melanin Responds to What You Eat, Drink, and Think 156

    Catch the Wave – *Chapter Summary*. *162*

Chapter 8: *Ignite the Internal Flames* 167

    Heaven and Earth 169

    Yoga and the Chakra System 172

    Activating the Engines 173

    Inspection of the Vessel 179

    Catch the Wave – *Chapter Summary*. *182*

PART THREE: ALL SYSTEMS GO **185**
    All Systems Go – Introduction 187

Chapter 9: *Sailing the High Seas* 189
    Prayer and Meditation 189
    Manifest the Life You Desire and Deserve 195
    From Victim to Victor 199
    Catch the Wave – *Chapter Summary* *202*

RISE and RAISE

RISE to Your Greatest Potential – RAISE the Collective Consciousness

EPILOGUE – THE RESURRECTION **207**
    Up, Up, You Mighty Race! 207
    7 Keys to the African American Resurrection Revisited 213

APPENDIX
    Bibliography 219
    Note from the Author/In Search of Self –
    The Resurrection of Our Name 221
    About the Author 225

LIST OF ILLUSTRATIONS

The Winter Solstice 45

Mayan Calendar 46

Mandala of Dendera 48

The Great Zodiac 49

The Great Galactic Alignment 51

The Zodiac Cycle 53

Is This Statue Solid? 66

An Atom 68

The Football Field 70

Settings on a Fan 89

The Seven Dimensions 93

Ascension/Descension 137

The Melanin Molecule 141

Water Crystals 161

The Chakra System 168

The Chakra Chart 170

The Brain Cell/The Universe 181

Foreword

ONCE EVERY FEW YEARS SOMEONE COMES ALONG THAT BLOWS everyone else out of the water. Brace yourselves for the unforgettable whirlwind that is Omiyale Jubé. In her latest work, *Navigate Your Existence! 7 Keys to the African American Resurrection,* she takes us on a journey of mythical proportions, shepherding us on a fascinating sojourn across the stars and back again. Indeed, you will travel from the projects…back to the pyramids…and on to the stars!

As Omiyale shares her story, we are catapulted back to a time that shaped many of our lives. A time when we found ourselves questioning who we are as a people. A time of light skin verses dark skin, good hair verses bad hair, big lips, big noses and big mama hips. Isn't it funny how many of us still find ourselves in that place of ridiculous separation? Many of us have gone through a learning process that has been slow and painful, looking deep inside struggling to overcome our feelings of self-hatred, and come to terms with our own prejudices. And yet, we have so far to go. Is this journey worth it, you ask? You bet it is and Omiyale takes us there, through the pain, the passion, the process to discover the truth and finally the triumph to "Know Thyself."

As Omiyale wakes us from our long, deep, profound sleep she hands us 7 keys to unlock our heads, hearts, and hands—returning the pride of our ancestry in the process.

In *Navigate Your Existence* we travel through the dimensions, compare and contrast Eastern and Western thought, explore energy, all bringing us to the Oneness and our connection to the All. We learn of the Laws of the cosmos, the wonders of Melanin and its power in our lives. We explore the chakras, blessed breath, our light bodies coming to the realization that the energy that connects us all resides within.

Omiyale is the consummate griot as she shares her stories, educating and imparting knowledge all the while. She has the ability to take highly complicated and complex concepts and break them down into simple bits and pieces for you to digest and make your own. She flings open the gates of understanding which catapults you on a journey of discovery and wonder. The best thing is that Omiyale accomplishes this rare feat with enthusiasm, clarity, power and a bit of humor that is all her own.

What a ride! As I read *Navigate Your Existence* with eagerness and relish then sat down to have a long conversation with Omiyale, I realized that this work is not only crucial to the African-American, this work is paramount for all of humanity.

The sharing of her personal story throughout and the knowledge revealed makes this a pivotal, pleasant, inspiring read. If you do nothing else for yourself, get comfortable in your favorite spot and read Omiyale Jube's *Navigate Your Existence! 7 Keys to the African American Resurrection* from cover to cover. Then, gift a copy to someone you care about—they will forever thank you, as I thank Omiyale for this splendid work.

Ashe

(And So It Is)

Colette 'IyaLe' Lundy
Founder of Harmony Pathways to Inner Balance
Harmony Pathways is a consortium of
women healers/practitioners.

Acknowledgements

With grace and gratitude I extend a heartfelt thank-you to:

The strong matriarchal trio from which I sprang forth:
My Great-Grandmother – Mama "Charlotte" Rucker
My Grandmother – Dorothy Evans
My Mother – Desdy Marshall

My first mentors who are responsible for my Cultural Awakening:
My Sister – Marcell Nydessa Pickett-Green
and
Anisa and G. Falcon Beazer

My family who supports me and shares me with the world:
DuShaun Johnson, Ahmad Johnson, Nyla Christian-Clark, Teombe Pickett Berry, David Green, Darriyante Johnson, and all the rest of my Grandchildren

Omiyale Jubé

All who nurtured and supported me through this process:

Earleana Giddings, Jonathan Fisher, Sandra Montalvo, Pamela Shepard, Mercedes Warrick, Sophia Flake, Leah Young, Collete Iyale Dill, Imani Shaw, Marcia Allen, and My Sisters in the Goddess Gathering,

A dear friend who thrust my metaphysical journey into forward motion:

Steven Giles

My Editor – Catherine Rourke

The host of Mentors—too numerous to mention—who have guided me, nurtured me, protected me, loved me…

Those living and those who have transitioned, known and unknown:

Ancestors, Spirit Guides, Guardian Angels, Ascended Masters, the Orisha, and the Almighty Divine Creator – The One.

I am eternally grateful for your guidance, support, and love.

Preface

**From the Pyramids to the Projects –
From the Projects to the Stars**

RELIEVED! I JUST FELT RELIEVED. A WONDERFUL FEELING OF serenity came over me. I had done it!

I had marched down the hall into the bathroom, opened the medicine cabinet, and drank from that bottle with the skull and crossbones marked "*poison*." Then, I waited. Soon the pain would be over.

I remember listening to the sirens of the ambulance arriving. The paramedics came into my bedroom where I sat patiently on the side of my bed. I heard them say they were taking me to Bellevue Hospital and a little concern entered my mind, since all New Yorkers knew that Bellevue, despite its excellent reputation, was a destination for the mentally insane. They rushed me to the Emergency Room and pumped my stomach—a truly unpleasant experience.

I was just nine years old, growing up in the projects of Harlem in New York. What could be so terrible as to make a nine-year-old girl want to end her life?

Well, I survived and am here to tell the story. Embedded within my story lie the secrets to a life of freedom, joy, happiness, and fulfillment of your dreams. I embarked upon this trek to share my story, hoping that some may learn from my struggles and tough lessons and maybe save years of unnecessary strife.

Early on in my young life, I was in so much pain that it caused me to want to end it all. This led me to becoming very sensitive to anyone who was exposed to hurt, pain, or suffering at any level. I became extremely empathetic, even at my young age.

As I grew older, I watched as my family and friends endured pain, injustice, and yes— even death. I watched and realized that there was no shortage of pain in the African American community. Much of this, if not all, was brought on by lack of knowledge. *"My people are destroyed for lack of knowledge."* Lack of knowledge of who we are; lack of knowledge about our past; lack of knowledge about the world we live in and how the universe works; lack of knowledge about the power we possess within. This lack of knowledge creates a gaping hole, leaving us swirling around in the unknown. Lost in a foreign culture, asleep to the knowledge of self.

So often we hear the cries to wake up and remember the past, to remember who we are. How can we be expected to wake up and know who we truly are when for centuries we've been led to believe we were someone or something else? It is difficult to expect such individuals to be aware of their past or greatness, having endured generations of suffering and "mis-education." Yet I am here to tell you that man was not meant to suffer. It is a matter of acquiring knowledge …the knowledge of self.

It is a matter of unlocking the secrets from our past that have been hidden from us in plain sight. Although the physical chains have been removed, we have experienced a mental, physical, and spiritual death. We have been asleep—metaphorically dead—for quite some time, and I say it is time to wake up. It is time for the *resurrection* of the African American mind, body, and soul.

My purpose for writing this book is to share my journey to liberation, my transformation from victim to victor. To share my experiences, my "aha" moments, and life lessons learned along the way that will provide you with a road map to empowerment, transformation, and yes—freedom.

Limiting Beliefs

There is a saying: "If you're not part of the solution, you're part of the problem." It's one of my favorite phrases, but I like to put a spin on it. If you don't *know* there is a problem, then you can't solve it, or even begin to search for a solution.

A critical first step in your process is to recognize what's holding you back from achieving the life you desire and deserve. What's weighing you down? What are the limiting beliefs that are keeping you from being the best you can be, reaching your greatest potential, or truly being free? I say a major culprit is a system of limiting beliefs that we have voluntarily or involuntarily incorporated into our lives.

How do you identify your limiting beliefs? What are they? Where do they come from? How do they show up in your life? I will delve deeper into limiting beliefs later on, while I provide both the answers and the solutions.

As I progressed in my understanding of our world, I learned that humanity at large is in pain and suffering. Humanity, in general, suffers from a victim mentality. Again, it is brought on by a lack of knowledge, by systems of limiting beliefs, and by the relinquishing of one's personal and spiritual power to the control of others.

So although this book is designed primarily for the African American populace, the information revealed within these pages is for the benefit of every man, woman, and child on this planet. After all, regardless of differences, we all come from the same source. Every human needs to be privy to this innovative and timely message. Every human has the right to exposure to the knowledge that can provide freedom to live the life he or she desires and deserves. Within these pages lie the secrets.

Moreover, what's important is that my suffering marked the beginning of a remarkable cultural and spiritual journey that would teach me how to become self-empowered, embrace a higher purpose, and navigate my existence.

In search of self, groping for the answers to my many questions and struggling to understand our world, I traveled both cultural and spiritual paths simultaneously. I wanted answers to questions such as: What are the guidelines we are supposed to live by? Why are we here? Who is God? Why? What? Who? When? and Where? This little girl had questions and no one to provide the answers—no answers that made sense, anyway.

But first, allow me to take you a little deeper into my story and the inspiration for writing this book and how it will help you navigate your own existence. After sharing my story with you, we will move on to identifying the limiting beliefs that prevent us from enjoying fulfilling lives.

Statistically, African Americans represent only 14 percent of the population of the United States, yet:

- Comprise nearly 50 percent of the population in the penal institutions;
- Comprise nearly 50 percent of the HIV/AIDS cases;
- Experience high percentages of disruptions to the family structure; and
- Experience high instances of low test scores and alarming drop-out rates.

Statistics like these led me to ask: How did we get from the Pyramids to the Projects? And…where do we go from here? Maybe we need to get back to the Pyramids (the knowledge of our ancestors) so we can move on to the Stars.

As an educator —both in the schools and in the community—I have spent most of my life teaching African American history and helping people reconnect with their cultural roots and understand our plight. But in these changing times, I truly believe that only through an awakening and an understanding of ourselves—individually and collectively, culturally as well as spiritually—will we be able to overcome the ills that presently haunt us as a people. And that's precisely why I wrote this book: to help other African Americans release themselves from the mental and spiritual *anchors of limitation* and acquire the knowledge of the ancestors, so that they too may experience true freedom and take control of their life's destination.

This leads to some profound questions that we need to be asking ourselves….

My mother always told me that if you have a question and can't get a satisfactory answer, keep it in the back of your head. One day you will discover the answer. I had lots of questions and very few answers.

What is it with this Black-White thing? Why does everything seem to revolve around race?

Why do they call us lazy, stupid, and ugly? Is it true?

Why is everything *black* associated with something bad…blacklist, blackballed, black market, etc.

Why do we have nappy hair?

Mommy, why am I Black?

And, if we built the Pyramids—how did we get from the Pyramids to the Projects?

Yes, I had questions, and no one could seem to supply satisfactory answers. I was too young to understand the system of white supremacy and racism, though I certainly was a recipient of the effects. It was not until I embraced my cultural heritage that the answers began to come and I started to find my place in the world.

In addition to becoming an educator by profession, I began a lifelong passion of teaching cultural heritage to the world from an Afrocentric perspective. The knowledge of my cultural heritage empowered me to have the confidence and self-esteem to pursue and achieve a successful life.

And yet, at some level, I still felt a sense of powerlessness—that others were in control of society and had control over me. The societal institutions were still Eurocentric in design.

Consequently, I felt a sense that, no matter how hard I worked to succeed, aspects of my life as a Black woman in America still remained in the hands of others, which instilled a feeling of being relegated to the status of a second-class citizen.

It wasn't until I took a philosophy course in college that I started to experience a series of "aha" moments that began answering my spiritual questions—information that led to my awareness that I was not relegated to second-class citizenship—that I was free to be and become anyone or anything I chose.

During the class I was introduced to the world of metaphysics—a world that we, as African Americans, were steered away from through the traditional church. We were told that anything associated with the metaphysical was "of the devil."

The term *metaphysics* was and still is today, in many circles, associated with the occult or anything that is hidden, secret, mysterious, and/or magical. The prefix "meta-" means *beyond*, so at a very basic level the word actually means *beyond the physical*, suggesting that there is something that exists other than that which we see or sense in our physical world. And therein lies many of the secrets to reclaiming our power and rightful place on this planet.

Through my exploration of metaphysics, I discovered the world of energy, Divine Consciousness, or that which many call *God*. It opened up a whole new frontier of exploration. I now had the universe at my fingertips, allowing me to experience spirituality from a different frame of reference.

This new information was mind-boggling, yet so simple! With each new "aha" moment, the answers to my questions kept flooding in. At first I believed this material to be contrary to what I was taught in school and church about the world and the universe. Later, I learned that this wisdom had similarities to the traditions in which I was raised, only viewed from a vastly different perspective. As I continued to increase my understanding of who I am, in addition to the world and the universe, the meaning of the adage "know thyself" became more and more profound.

"My people are destroyed for lack of knowledge." Yes, Know Thyself! Knowledge *is* power. With a newly-acquired understanding of the world, the universe, and how it all works came more profound answers to my questions.

Again, my quest for answers took me along two routes—one cultural and one spiritual—and the paths crossed and intertwined over the years. My cultural path was invaluable to me, and learning about my great heritage gave me my first reason to live. This cultural knowledge instilled a sense of worthiness and self-esteem …a sense of pride.

Over the years the answers kept pouring in, expanding my horizons. Now, more of my spiritual questions were being answered. My world was transforming right before my eyes. So many people were groping for answers to these very same questions, and many still have not found the answers. With a purpose inspired by higher forces, I knew I had to find a venue to share the secrets and help others to navigate life's course, without all the pain and suffering. Or at the very least, provide individuals the knowledge and tools necessary to navigate the many obstacles and challenges life throws their way and do so from a position of power …with a sense of calm, resolve, and control.

- Are you searching for answers to life's existence?
- Do you wonder why you are here and what your purpose is?
- Do you have religious questions that nobody can answer?
- Do you have questions you are afraid to ask in church?
- Are you seeking more from life…more wealth, more health, and more spiritual enlightenment?
- Are you searching for a better way, with an innate sense that there is far more to life than what has been presented to you or than meets the eye?
- Given the times we are in, are you simply wondering… WHAT IN THE WORLD IS GOING ON?

Then this book is for you!

The purpose of this book is to facilitate the awareness that you already possess everything you need to navigate your existence, which requires you to take control of your life's destination. This, in turn, requires you to transform from victim to victor, which requires a resurrection of the mind, body, and soul and results in ultimate freedom.

Navigate Your Existence is designed to open new portals of understanding for those who would like to unlock the secrets and take control of their personal and spiritual lives. It provides a foundation of information that everyone needs in order to comprehend how the Law of Attraction and "The Secret" work. Its mission is to teach people how to discover and ignite their internal energies in order to rise to their peak potential on the journey to self-empowerment, self-actualization, and personal transformation. The book takes the "mystique" out of metaphysics. It affords you the tools necessary to take control of your life's destination so you may enjoy physical, personal, spiritual, and financial success.

I find myself on a mission to provide knowledge to set into motion the resurrection of the African American mind, body, and soul. This is knowledge that every African American must know to restore us as a people to the greatness that once was ours.

It is my belief that every African American already possesses everything he or she needs for the transformation from victim to victor. Within these pages lie the 7 Keys to the African American Resurrection. Unlock the secrets to personal and spiritual freedom; take control of your life's destination and achieve the life you desire and deserve!

It is also my belief that as we rise as a people, so too will humanity rise, for there is only one universal consciousness. It is my greatest desire that as each individual rises to his or her peak potential, each will find ways to serve humanity and raise the collective consciousness.

There are many African Americans who need to take the cultural journey and learn about our great heritage. Many of us still need to learn the African origins of civilization, the truth about the slave trade, and the numerous contributions of African Americans to American society, in addition to understanding the oppressive system of white supremacy and how we came to our current situation.

I cannot stress enough the importance of making this a matter of *utmost* priority in your life. There is an abundance of information and resources at your fingertips to teach you about your story, and more importantly, about your greatness. All you have to do is look. Until you do, you will not know the tremendous sense of pride that awaits you. Nor can you function at your greatest ability, aspiring to be other than who you are.

Although discussions of our plight are addressed throughout, ***discovering your cultural roots is not the purpose of this book.***

The times we find ourselves in dictate a need to expound on the spiritual aspect of my discoveries. Thus we will spend more time along the spiritual (metaphysical) leg of my journey because, as I uncovered the secrets within the world of metaphysics, the more profound my transformation from victim to victor became.

The more I learned about the powers of the universe, the more I realized that each of us is responsible for *and in control of* our own lives. We create our own reality. Until we learn these truths and incorporate this knowledge into our lives, we will remain victims and mentally enslaved.

We do not have to wait for anyone to remove the shackles from our minds that keep us enslaved, nor wait for someone to save us. Knowledge IS power. As you learn of the magnificent world of energy that abounds in the universe and within you, you will be empowered with the tools to transform your world.

Within these pages are the keys to the transformation of your mind, body, and soul from victim to victor. So, this book will assist you in moving from the feelings on the left—that of a victim—to the actualizations on the right—those of a victor.

From feelings of:

Pain	to	Resolve
Anger	to	Calm
Blame	to	Responsibility
Hurt	to	Being Healed
Powerless	to	Powerful
Controlled	to	Being in Control

As an African American living in America, many of the conditions that affect my world are of great concern to me. However, I now possess the tools to view these situations from a totally different realm.

More importantly, I now act upon these issues with new resolve. I no longer have to maintain a victim mentality, languishing in pain, anger, blaming others, or still feeling powerless and controlled. I now have the tools to take responsibility for my life. I now know how to transform my world and existence to that of a victor, reacting from a position of responsibility and control. And I will show you in this book how you can achieve that too.

Furthermore, being in control means that, finally, we as a people can break the chains and experience mental, physical, and spiritual FREEDOM. Some may call it salvation; I call it liberation—a resurrection of the mind, body, and soul brought on by the acquisition of knowledge of SELF.

Eventually, the knowledge acquired through my cultural and spiritual paths crossed and became one and the same. Know that this information can be obtained through either path if you trace it back to its origins. If you study your cultural heritage, it will lead you to Egyptology, which will encompass the study of metaphysics. If you study the spiritual path, it too will lead back to Kemet/Egypt. (*Kemet* is the original name before it was changed to *Egypt* by the Greeks). The path you choose is up to you. The important thing is to begin. So, for this journey, we will discuss aspects of both paths but focus mainly on the "aha" moments of my spiritual journey. As we uncover the secrets, you will unleash the awesome powers you have at your disposal that can transform your personal and spiritual life.

"Is it time to take the Red Pill?"

Of course, this is a reference to the movie, *The Matrix*. Wikipedia describes it this way: "The film depicts a future in which reality as perceived by most humans is actually a simulated reality created by sentient machines to pacify and subdue the human population, while their bodies' heat and electrical activity are used as an energy source. Upon learning this, computer programmer 'Neo' is drawn into a rebellion against the machines, involving other people who have been freed from the 'dream world' and into reality."

Take the Blue Pill to remain in the "dream world," which for many of us means to remain mentally and spiritually enslaved. Take the Red Pill to return to what IS. Neo chose the Red Pill and *realized* he possessed amazing powers and untold potential. It was a matter of making a choice and becoming aware…consciously.

We, too, have a choice. We, too, possess amazing powers and untold potential. It is time to discover a world that has been hidden from us and to uncover the secrets to creating our own reality, the one we desire. If we change our thinking, we change our world. How exciting!

From the Pyramids to the Projects, and from the Projects to the Stars. It is certainly time to leave the Projects and "Move on Up," as was so eloquently presented to us by "The Jeffersons." By first returning to the Pyramids and the knowledge of the ancestors, we will acquire that spark necessary to ignite the resurrection of our mind, body, and soul. It will create that vehicle of consciousness that will ultimately take us to the Stars.

So the question becomes: "What now? What's in it for me? Why should I take time out of my already too-busy schedule to read this book?" Times have changed. The old ways of dealing with situations are no longer working. It's time to find a new direction and make a shift in the paradigm. I will take you on a journey and cover topics that will force you out of your comfort zone. And that's all right. It is time to explore new horizons.

You will learn:

All about the end of the Mayan Calendar and beyond 2012—the implications and how they affect you

- Lifestyle changes necessary to transition through these momentous times
- End-of-the-world prophecies versus end-of-an-era documentation

- What's in store for humanity, our planet, and the universe
- How you can utilize free energy sources to enhance your health, happiness, and connection to God
- How to utilize this information to increase your wealth and finances
- How to harness the forces of the universe to take control of your personal and spiritual destination
- Answers for those seeking ascension and spiritual enlightenment
- And so much more

Over the years, I've spent hours upon hours, months and years researching this information, which has prepared me for the task at hand. I've traveled to the motherland visiting Kemet/Egypt with the renown Egyptologist, Dr. Ben Jochannan. I've traveled extensively in Europe. I've read numerous books spanning a wide range of topics from history to science, and on to metaphysics. I've delved into the so-called "mysteries," which I call MY Story—the story of the ancient ones…your ancestors.

Furthermore, I've been blessed to have had the benefit of many mentors over the years, some renowned, some not so famous, but dear friends and acquaintances. I currently travel in circles with many enlightened persons from whom I am able to glean new and profound information all the time. I've been trained in Reiki, yoga, meditation, and healing techniques. In addition, as one who seeks knowledge, information just seems to find me. Being in the right place at the right time has led to many of my "aha" moments that transformed my life. The fact that you are reading this book means you are right where you need to be and at just the right time.

It is my greatest desire that sharing my journey of "aha" moments that transformed my life will lead you along your own path of exploration. When you are finished reading this book, you will have the 7 Keys to the African American Resurrection, unlocking the secrets to transform your life to a self-empowered victor. It is an honor for me to share this profound wisdom with you so that you, too, can navigate your way to a healthier, happier, and more fulfilled life. Together we will set sail on a voyage of amazing discovery.

In the ensuing chapters, as you ingest the message within, you will realize that we—all of humanity—are connected. All of humanity is connected to the heartbeat of the Earth. All of humanity shares one universal conscious mind and experiences the divine flow of the universe. I look forward to the day when all of humanity can live in the peace, balance, and harmony of the One Universal Source: The All.

So, come and take the journey, uncovering the secrets that will enable you to discover your internal compass, chart your course of destination, and Navigate Your Existence!

Introduction

Conductor of the Ship

We don't receive wisdom; we must discover it for ourselves after a journey that no one can take for us, or spare us. –Marcel Proust

PICTURE THIS: THE POSTMAN ARRIVES AT YOUR DOOR WITH A certified letter. Upon opening the letter, you find that you are the owner of a magnificent ship. It's yours, free and clear, to do with what you will—take a trip, and/or travel to untold destinations.

Can you visualize your ship? Are you excited? Good! Are you ready for your journey?

Let's explore some ideas you might need to consider:
- Who's conducting the ship?
- What's the ship's destination?
- In which direction must it travel to get there?
- Is the ship prepared for the journey? Is it cleaned, oiled, fueled?
- Has the course been charted?

Do these inquiries make you want to step back and consider some major preparations?

Well, what if I told you that you already have a ship, a magnificent vessel, and that vessel is <u>you</u>? The physical you—your body! Now with that in mind, ask yourself these questions again. Who's conducting *your* ship? Or, is it being steered by someone else's plan for you? Who's at the helm in your life?

Where are you headed? Do you have a destination? And…In what direction is your compass pointing?

Has your course been charted? Do you have the necessary knowledge and tools to Navigate Your Existence?

If you answered "no" to any of the above—congratulations! You are in the right place at the right time. The message of this book is intended to expose you to the information needed to enable you to *Discover Your Internal Compass* and *Set Sail to Untold Destinations*. So let's begin.

Each of us has a ship or vessel—our physical body—and an energy source or life force that conducts the vessel. Thus I use the term "Conductor of the Ship" versus a "captain," who is a chief or leader. I want to equip you with the tools necessary to be the "Conductor" of your life's destination and the "Conductor" of your energy—the life force which, in essence, is you!

Preparing you to take the helm—the wheel and the rudder—and take "charge" of your ship requires viewing our world from a different perspective. My intention is to share my journey with you—one that was inspired by experiences and "aha" moments that completely changed my perspectives on how I viewed life, this world, and the universe. This new perspective is not necessarily different from how I was brought up, but it is certainly viewed through different lenses.

That's why the book begins with my story, so you can see how this whole journey unfolded and why my experience created the blueprint for the foundation of this book.

But first let's establish some ground rules, or do a little housekeeping. As I share my experiences, you may hear some familiar concepts—some that you've never heard before and others that you disagree with, don't believe, or are simply not willing to accept. And that's just fine. My job here is not to make anybody a believer. I can only share my experience, my beliefs, some resources, and encourage you to exercise your own due diligence.

This is the story of my truth—that which I believe to be true today. As I continue to learn and expand my knowledge base, so too will my truth expand and ultimately shift in certain perspectives. During your journey or quest, you will discover your truth, that which fits and is just right for you.

Do not believe in anything simply because you have heard it. Do not believe in anything simply because it is spoken and rumored by many. Do not believe in anything simply because it is found written in your religious books. Do not believe in anything merely on the authority of your teachers and elders. Do not believe in traditions because they have been handed down for many generations. But after observation and analysis, when you find that anything agrees with reason and is conducive to the good and benefit of one and all, then accept it and live up to it. **–Buddha**

While speaking about perspectives, I am sure that many readers come from wide and diverse religious backgrounds—from Christianity, Judaism, and Islam —and adhere to other beliefs such as Buddhism, Hindu and/or Yoruba. And there are those who consider themselves New Age, New Thought, or even Atheist.

This work is not intended to be religious in nature, although many times I will refer to adages common in various religions, spiritual practices, and philosophies. In addition, often I will make references to the God Source, God Source Energy, Divine Consciousness, the One, the All, etc. It is my assumption that many people believe that there is only one "Source" or one "God," which is known to people by many different names. In these instances, if you prefer to interject the name that you use to refer to your God, or infinite source, please do so.

Some of the concepts shared here may be new and therefore they challenge us to move out of our comfort zone, leaving us feeling a little anxious.

My intention is to share some knowledge that I have acquired along my path— knowledge that is not mine to claim. That is to say, this knowledge has come to me by way of experiences, mentors, books, and other means. As I mentioned before, knowledge just seems to find me. Many times when I am searching for an answer, the right book just seems to show up.

Again, my mother said to keep those questions that no one seems to have the answers to in the "back of your head," and the answers will appear. There's something to be said about the adage, "Seek and ye shall find."

Much of the information within this book came to me little by little, over a span of many years. It took me years of studying and growth to comprehend each topic to the extent of my present understanding. I, too, am still on the path of enlightenment, with so much yet to learn. I am but a student myself, with a yearning to share my lessons thus far.

No one journey is the same. As voyagers you will experience the information in a manner that is personal and unique to you. Every topic explored is a profound concept in and of itself, with vast amounts of information available to research. With each chapter you will find the concepts building on each other, each helping to provide a more profound understanding of the previous information.

You will also find the information repeated from time to time. That is because the material overlaps. The content of each chapter, however different, stems from the same source—that which connects us all, the oneness. It is my intention to introduce each concept, share my experience, and then allow you to embark on your own journey of exploration.

Each one of you will have to find your comfort zone and then allow yourself to *step outside* of it. As you are introduced to new concepts, you create and open neuropathways in your brain. It is said that once a rubberband has been stretched, it can never go back to its original size. Expand your horizons. Ask the questions you've always wanted to ask and enjoy your quest to find the answers.

Ship Ahoy!

All great navigators know that navigation is a process. It entails completing a number of tasks before casting off, such as planning, preparation, etc. Thus our journey unfolds in three separate segments.

First, one must begin by gathering any and all information required during the course of the voyage. Hence, **Part One** is titled: "**CHART THE COURSE – Gathering the Information**."

Next in the order of importance is the need to prime your vessel for optimal performance, or get it into tip-top shape. This necessitates inspection of the vessel, cleaning and fueling, and revving up the engines. Accordingly, **Part Two** is: "**START THE ENGINES – Preparation for Optimal Performance**."

Finally, you are ready to put all of your hard work into full swing and set everything in motion. Therefore, **Part Three** is: "**All SYSTEMS GO – Getting Underway**."

And now you are UNDERWAY, traveling toward your destination.

Now that we've got our nautical course of action in place, it's time to focus on the 7 Keys to the African American Resurrection. Each key, in and of itself, is quite simple. Yet, each requires work, discipline, commitment, study, practice, and on and on. Just like anything worth having, is worth working for.

The Ankh is the Kemetic/Egyptian Symbol for The Key of Life

The **7 KEYS** are as follows:

RECOGNIZE – The Anchors of Limitation
In order to solve a problem, one must first recognize there is a problem and identify the source.

RESTORE – The Knowledge of the Ancestors
There is nothing new under the sun. The ancestors knew the secrets to the universe. They had the answers, and that knowledge is buried within your core.

RESPONSIBILITY – Take Responsibility

RELEASE –the Anchors
You create your own reality. Take Responsibility for your life in every thought, action and deed. Free yourself from past baggage…Release the Anchors

REACTIVATE – Your Energy Sources
You have the power within. It is up to you to reactivate your sources of power.

RECLAIM – Your Power
Manifest the personal and spiritual life you desire and deserve

☥ RISE and RAISE

RISE – to Your Greatest Potential and
RAISE – the Collective Consciousness

RISE

The comprehension of and dedication to the 7 Keys result in heightened awareness. As your awareness rises, so too will your vibration, your spirit, your consciousness. As you Rise in consciousness, so too will your ability to Rise to your Greatest Potential

RAISE

As you rise, you inevitably affect the surrounding environment. As you rise and Raise your consciousness, in turn you Raise the consciousness of African American people, Raise the consciousness of humanity, and Raise the consciousness of the planet. It is your duty to RISE and thereby RAISE the Collective Consciousness.

Well, there you have it— the 7 Keys to the African American Resurrection. As previously stated, the keys, in and of themselves, are relatively simple. However, it is through the implementation of each key where the serious work becomes evident. Hence, the journey through the chapters will unfold the secrets to executing the keys. As we noted before, anything worth having is worth working for.

Utilizing a nautical theme and incorporating the 7 Keys will lay out a system to impart the knowledge and tools needed to steer you toward a liberation of your mind, body, and soul, providing the tools necessary to take control of your life's destination.

This can mean tools for how to empower yourself to get that new job or new house. Or it could provide techniques to safely transition these turbulent times, or teach you how you raise your vibration so your sojourn through these times offers smooth sailing. For some it will mean spiritual growth and enlightenment, so you enjoy a closer relationship to that which you call God.

There is quite a bit of information to cover as we make our way through the waves. Some material will be familiar to you and some not so much as we delve into the questions regarding life's mysteries. It is my intention to make seemingly difficult concepts more palatable to digest.

Again, the concepts overlap and build on each other so that, as we continue, each one will become clearer and easier to understand.

Each chapter ends in a Catch the Wave summary which includes: **Important Points to Remember, Action Steps,** and **Life Lessons for Transformation**. "Important Points to Remember" is designed as a review of significant aspects of the chapter. The "Action Steps" portion provides direction for those asking: "Now what?? What am I supposed to do with all of this information and where do I start?"

The "Action Steps" component lists suggestions to get moving in the right direction. The Action Steps are not designed as a to-do list in which one tries to complete each and every step. Rather, it is a list of suggestions to apply the knowledge acquired within the chapter. Some activities you may want to incorporate into your lifestyle immediately. By way of contrast, you might prefer to read the book in its entirety, then focus on the action steps. Here again, you have choice; focus on a few items in each chapter, or concentrate on one chapter at a time.

However you choose to apply the information matters not. What does matter is that you *act*! The "Life Lessons for Transformation" section includes anecdotal stories explaining how this information affected me personally, how it spurred on the transformation in my life, and how it can assist you to effect change in your life.

The secrets uncovered through my process of evolution presented invaluable lessons. The information within these pages is powerful and life-changing. And it works, but only if you work it.

Also, just in case some of you might feel like I'm stepping on a few toes as we encounter some stormy seas in certain sections, please keep in mind that I'm simply sharing information. It is not my intention to seem judgmental or point fingers at anyone. I, too, am in the process of rethinking how I maintain my ship. And it is just that—a process. The important thing is that we learn what's needed for transformation and begin somewhere.

Likewise, you will encounter some high seas from time to time when some of the information becomes a little technical or scientific. As a teacher, I used to tell my students, "Lessons can be fun and interesting, but sometimes we just have to cover the hard stuff." Remember that the lessons build on each other. As you continue on, the waves will part, and you will be able to see your way clearly to the shore.

So…don't jump ship! Hang in there with me throughout the entire journey. At the end of the voyage, immense light will shine through your prism, enabling you to view your world through new perspectives and taking you to untold destinations.

And that's exactly what we will be doing here together. But first, in order to help you prepare for the journey, let's begin with my stormy saga….

PART ONE

Chart The Course
Gathering the Information

The Scarab Beetle
Kemetic/Egyptian Symbol of Resurrection

Chart The Course

Gathering the Information

Introduction

THE JOURNEY HAS COMMENCED. YOU HAVE INITIATED THE VOYAGE. Now it is up to you to chart the course.

Just like any journey, sometimes the road gets bumpy, or there may be turbulence along the way. Maybe a wave pushed you back, or shifted you off course. You may have to pull out the charts or do some more research to keep the ship on course.

My mother always told me that, no matter where you're headed or how far it is, you can't get there unless you start. In this section we'll be gathering the information required to set sail.

Each of us is on our own personal journey—each starting out at a different place. Decide where you're at right now; you will know. Your intuition—that inner voice—will tell you. Depending on where you are in your journey, this information may seem overwhelming. How do you eat an elephant? One bite at a time.

The universe is in exact order. We are all right where we are supposed to be. Also, be mindful of the times we are in. There is a sense of urgency to get the ship-a-sailing toward your destination. Time really is flying and you cannot recover time that is wasted.

So to give you some momentum and inspiration for your journey, let's start with mine. It has taken me a lifetime to reach this point, over many years of seeking answers, researching, and experiencing my "aha" moments, which you are about to hear in a moment. I've had numerous mentors and I'm grateful to each and every one of them. While they have taught me so much, I still have so much yet to learn.

Here, now, is my story.

RECOGNIZE the Anchors of Limitation

Chapter 1

My Story: The Journey Begins

The Journey Begins

My journey began with a quest, searching for answers. Answers to questions from different paths in my life—one cultural and another spiritual.

The questions generated from the cultural path emerged from the pain of being Black in America, a truly painful experience. I endured the trauma, the worthlessness brought on by the residual effects of slavery and the continued system of racism in America. That being said, we'll begin the story here.

Growing Up Black in America

A typical day for me, "Cookie," consisted of beatings from my mother, physical and mental abuse from my brother and sister, and feelings of worthlessness from the elementary school I attended.

My mother was a phenomenal woman, although overburdened and stressed as a single parent of three. She often worked two and sometimes three jobs. She was determined to be a good parent and have her children "turn out right." Prior to leaving for work, she prepared the list of chores for each of us to be completed by the time she returned from work.

I wasn't a bad kid or particularly mischievous; I just couldn't complete my chores. Playing with my brother's battleship, equipped with airplanes and missiles, or his train set with the smoke coming out of the smokestack, interested me much more than …ironing clothes.

In fact, there was always something more interesting to do—anything rather than my chores. So, like clockwork my mother would arrive home from work, put down her purse, take off her shoes, check to see if "Cookie" had completed her chores, then commence to beating my butt! It was a ritual, five to six times a week—every week. Hard to believe, but true.

Every year my sister, brother, and I would get to ride the Amtrak train "Down South" and stay with our family in North Carolina for the summer. I was the youngest of the three siblings. Unlike my sister and brother, my complexion was lighter, thus I was considered "light-skinned." Consequently, I was highly favored by my relatives. I received special treatment over my sister, and sometimes my brother was even mistreated on my behalf.

Upon returning north to New York, my sister and brother spent the rest of the year getting their retribution. My sister tortured me mentally, and my brother felt obligated to inflict some type of physical abuse upon me on a daily basis. Afraid of consequences from my brother and sister, I never told my mother about the mental and physical abuse, and it continued for years. Eventually, my mother found out about the preferential treatment in the South and the annual trips ceased.

Wanting the best for her children, my mother decided that we were not going to attend the school behind the building for the

"Project kids." As you might imagine, the school had a predominantly Black student population and low standards—along with low expectations. Instead, we attended the school up the hill with the White students, more affluent Black students, and some of the students from the Projects.

Of course the teachers were predominately White. I remember feeling somewhat out of place, especially during the history lessons, since it was quite apparent that I didn't resemble anyone in the history books. All of the references to persons contributing to civilization were White.

Oh, except for the one paragraph about slavery. Every year when we reached that paragraph, I just wanted to crawl under the desk with embarrassment. Finally, the *only* reference to someone who resembled me and it was in regards to my being a descendent from slaves. It resulted in me feeling inferior and ashamed of being Black.

Every year, when it was time to read that one paragraph, I just wanted to be invisible. In addition, I received taunts of "Black, ugly, and bald-headed" from the students. Obviously, it didn't matter that I was light-skinned.

All of the aforementioned situations occurred on a daily basis. This was my life, day after day after day—the mental and physical abuse, the beatings, the torment, and feelings of worthlessness. At nine years old, I wanted it to end. I couldn't take it anymore, so I took matters into my own hands. I marched down that hallway, opened the medicine cabinet, found that bottle with the skull and cross bones on it marked "Poison," and attempted suicide.

I can remember that day as if it was yesterday. I even remember what I was wearing—those white capris pants with the purple designs on them. Thank goodness I wasn't successful, and I'm here to tell the story.

My life really didn't change much until about three years later. That's when the beatings and physical and mental abuse stopped. My mother just gave up, because I was never known to get my chores done. In addition, as I grew taller and bigger than both my sister and brother, they made the better choice to leave me alone once and for all. Yay!

But the pain of being Black in America continued. I watched as the drugs crept into my neighborhood. Black people couldn't find jobs; more and more people became welfare recipients; and Blacks were portrayed in the media with negative stereotypes as criminals or just good for nothing.

I didn't understand. The effects showed up in my life as low self-esteem, feelings of worthlessness, poor grades, apathy, and a grim outlook for the future.

At the time I had no idea that my physical and mental pain stemmed from being Black in America. I had no idea that the beatings, the issues surrounding favoritism of lighter skin, the disdain for darker skin, and the feelings of worthlessness were all rooted in the history of slavery, racism, and white supremacy in America.

Stripped of our African culture and heritage, much of the current socialization for Black people is a direct result of centuries of slavery and racial discrimination. How we interface with our families and with each other in our communities today stems from the disconnect of ancestral values, how we have been treated, and the assimilation into cultural values other than our own.

The dehumanization and trauma of slavery and discrimination devastated African American families and their spirits. Under the system of slavery attempting to practice or hold onto any remnants of spiritual or cultural traditions resulted in harsh punishment or beatings. Over the years, African Americans "adopted," so to speak, beatings into the child-rearing practices. This practice continues today as the Black family struggles to regain the cultural mores of its ancestors.

Color discrimination was not just practiced between Blacks and Whites. As a Black person, the "shade" of your skin further determined the degree of discrimination leveled against you by both the White and Black communities. In other words, the lighter your skin, the more preferential treatment you received.

This was certainly the case during slavery, and it continues on to this very day. As we struggled to assimilate into the Eurocentric-American society, Blacks with lighter skin and European features were more likely to succeed. This further fueled a color divide within the Black community. The implications of color discrimination crept into my childhood, affected my life tremendously, and caused serious consequences.

Through slavery, the distortion of true African history, and being stripped of our African culture and heritage, we have lost knowledge of self, resulting in feelings of inferiority, loss of self-esteem, and pride for ourselves as a people. Although physical slavery ended, the conditions have not changed a great deal in the hearts and minds of much of America.

"What happens when a group of people are kidnapped from their homes, smuggled away in chains, and held captive in a foreign land, where they are tortured, raped, and forced to perform hard labor by the lash of a whip and under the constant threat of death?"

This is but one of the issues addressed by Sultan A. Latif and Naimah Latif in their awesome book, *SLAVERY: The African American PSYCHIC TRAUMA,* in which they content that African Americans suffer from psychic trauma resulting from "The monstrous legacy of slavery." As we continue to uncover the truth concerning our current state of affairs, understanding the concept of African American psychic trauma is a must.

As a child, I had no knowledge of the concept of psychic trauma, but I was aware that Black people were still trapped in a mental system of slavery. Subtle (and not-so-subtle) messages that rendered Black people as second-class citizens were still present in everyday existence. These surfaced not only when I was at school, but also right in my neighborhood on the streets of Harlem. Even as a child, it was not so easy to escape the feelings of worthlessness, or just not being *good* enough.

I survived the suicide attempt and resumed living my life, but it was an existence of the culturally dead. Lost to knowledge of self… living day to day with no purpose or direction. Certainly I could not claim to be navigating my existence. And then it happened: the initiation of my cultural awakening.

My Cultural Awakening

My sister belonged to an organization called *Karma, The Living Workshop*, which was founded by G. Falcon Beazer, known to many as "G." Its mission was to provide knowledge on "How to Survive in the 21st Century." G's premise advocated that people be participants on the "Stage of Life"—in other words, encouraging and providing a venue for people to engage actively in life, as opposed to being an observer.

"The Life Players" was a troupe that evolved as an offshoot from *Karma the Living Workshop.*

The Life Players was comprised of Black historians, poets (including the renowned "Last Poets"), artists, musicians, dancers, etc. They traveled across New York City and nearby areas, teaching African and African American Heritage.

I was just sixteen when my sister and her friend, Anisa, inducted me into the group to assist with the African fashion shows. I learned so much about my heritage that summer that it changed my life. No, it saved my life, for now I had something to live for. For the first time I felt a sense of pride and a sense of worthiness. I discovered that I *do* have a culture, and a history; my history does *not* begin in this country as a slave.

My life took on a whole new direction. I began to excel in school, went on to college, and achieved great success in life. From that experience, I realized the importance of knowing who you are—"Know Thyself." I began to study Black history and practice the celebration of Kwanzaa.

Many of the answers to my questions were acquired by reading books such as *Nile Valley Contributions to Civilizations* by Anthony Browder; *100 Amazing Facts About The Negro With Complete Proof* by J. A. Rogers; and *What They Never Told You in History Class* by Indus Khamit-Kush.

Knowledge of self on a physical-cultural realm is imperative. One must have a reason to exist and be productive. This is crucial for persons of African American descent for several reasons.

One, it is necessary to know our ancestral history and the many contributions of our people to civilization to combat the negative stereotypes and "mis-education." We live in a world in which we are bombarded with negative messages every day (some subtle, some not so subtle). These messages tell us that we are not worthy, that our people have not contributed anything of substance to the civilized world, and that we are lazy, stupid, and ugly. The very color associated with our people is a negative term in the English language: black market, blacklist, black mark, black or dark day, etc. The negative stereotypical character of African Americans portrayed in the media continues to invade the airwaves. I could go on for a while, but you get the picture. After all you are living it.

This negative image is further substantiated as African Americans bought into the hatred of self and low self-esteem, along with so many other variables. We no longer have to fear someone else portraying negative images of us on the screens. We supply the images ourselves, reflective in much of our music, videos, and movies.

There is a wonderful book titled *Mis-Education of the Negro*, by Carter G Woodson. It speaks to the phenomenon of perpetual slave mentality. Woodson writes:

If you can control a man's thinking, you do not have to worry about his action. When you determine what a man shall think, you do not have to concern yourself about what he will do. If you make a person feel inferior, you do not have to compel him/her to accept an inferior status, he/she will seek for it. If you make a person think that he/she is justly an outcast, you do not have to order that person to the back door, that person will go without being told, and if there is no back door, the very nature of that person will demand one.

Profound words written so long ago that affected me when I first read them, yet they ring true still today. Again, it is imperative that we African Americans embrace our cultural heritage and come into the Knowledge of Self. It was such a crucial step in my journey.

I was always very positive about the struggle and progress of our people. I hate to admit it, but there came a time when I began to question our very existence as a people on this planet. It made me work that much harder to teach African American history, Egyptology, and the celebration of Kwanzaa. I knew the benefits of learning my history and how it transformed my life. I always believed that knowledge of our history—Knowledge of Self—was the answer to our survival.

Learning my history awarded me a new lease on life. I gained a sense of worthiness, a sense of self-esteem, and a sense of pride. Learning about my rich heritage provided the impetus to be a success in life. With a new sense of self, I increased my grades in high school, went on to college, and became a professional in the field of education.

Yet, I still felt like a second-class citizen, living in a European-dominated society. I still felt as if something was missing; more importantly, I didn't feel free.

The freedom I was looking for came much later in my quest for spiritual answers. So let's begin that leg of my journey.

My Spiritual Journey – *Why Are We Here?*

My quest for spiritual understanding also began early in life. Being raised in a traditional Baptist church in Harlem often meant spending the entire day at church. Generally, my family arrived at church early in the morning for Sunday school, attended Sunday service, and stayed for evening service.

Usually, my grandmother would attend church meetings between Sunday service and evening service, which meant I had plenty of time to ask the church ladies my questions. And you know I had questions. Unfortunately, I could not seem to get any satisfactory answers.

I wanted to know:

How can God be everywhere at the same time?

Why does God let bad things happen to good people?

Is the world really coming to an end?

And…

Why can't I wear pants for the church outing to Hersey Amusement Park next Sunday?

I would get responses like "It's just not ladylike to wear pants."

But you would prefer my dress fly over my head on the roller coaster? It made no sense to me.

Or I'd get responses like "God knows best," or "Only God knows," and "You'll get your reward in heaven." It was these types of answers that drove me away from the church. Many people are still asking some of these questions today. Sooo…again, I listened to my mother and kept my questions tucked away in the "back of my head."

Without the church to provide moral guidance, what was I going to use to determine my behavior and promote sound judgment? After all, I was deathly afraid of not getting into heaven.

As a little girl, I had the wisdom to select the Golden Rule as my moral framework: "Do unto others as you shall have others do unto you." This made perfect sense to me. All people wanted to be treated fairly.

To that extent, I figured if I was as good as I could be and treated people fairly, I'd be allowed into the gates of heaven. I continued on for years utilizing the Golden Rule as my guide and moral standard for life—my golden compass.

However, it would be many years later before the answers to my spiritual questions began to surface. I knew there was more to the story than what I was being told in the church. This next experience led me to know beyond any doubt that there was more to life than meets the eye. It was the beginning of my higher awareness.

A Doorway to Higher Awareness

Initially, my first encounter with the concept *"Life After Life"* began with the phone ringing in my dorm room early one morning at the State University of New York at Stony Brook. I stumbled to the phone and someone on the other end said, "I've got bad news—Mother died." Now this was my grandmother whom I loved dearly. I was quite upset, but I managed to gather my bags and make my way into the city.

My grandmother was a taxicab driver in New York City and oftentimes worked late and awkward hours, so she had a habit of falling asleep most anywhere—on the couch, in a chair, or the floor. She could get comfortable almost anywhere.

It seems that my grandmother had a stroke and fell on the floor. As she lay there resting her head on one arm, she appeared to be sleeping. As people began to arrive at her house, the moment we saw her lying seemingly in a comfortable sleeping position, all of the hurt and sadness left. This enabled me to accept my grandmother's death—that she was gone and I'd never see her again. And I was all right with that.

However, that night while I was lying in my bed, my attention was drawn to the upper right-hand corner of the room. I didn't see or hear anything. But I knew it was my grandmother. A calm came over me as she let me know she was just fine. From that day on, I just knew that "when you die, you're not really dead." It was the beginning of my understanding of an afterlife. The experience provided a doorway to higher awareness—a gateway to new understandings. Yet, many years passed before I had the opportunity to revisit this concept on a more profound level.

As mentioned earlier, it was not until I took a philosophy course in college and was introduced to metaphysics that I began to experience a series of the "aha" moments and receive answers to my spiritual questions.

At any rate, my experience with my grandmother heightened my awareness to the unseen world, making me aware that there was more than what I was being told and more than meets the eye.

Which brings me to the "aha" moment in my life that took me to the next level of "when you die, you're not really dead" or *Life After Life.*

Life After Life

To the world at large, it appeared that I was living the American Dream. Although I was married and had the house, two cars, two kids, great job, and the works, my dream contained some flaws. An average day consisted of cooking, cleaning, working a full-time job, and taking care of two infants and a husband. I thought I was starring in the commercial for Virginia Slims. Some of you may remember the lines from that 1970's commercial: *I can bring home the bacon, fry it up in a pan, and never let you forget you're a man. 'Cause I'm a woman.* Well I was Virginia and Superwoman all wrapped up in one!

My days started off at 4 a.m., getting two babies ready for the babysitters, including lunches and baby bags, getting myself ready for work, then delivering both babies to two different locations, before I headed in a third direction for my job. At the end of my workday, I again traveled to two different locations to pick up my sons before heading home. Once I hit the door, I started my evening routine. Get the babies settled, start fixing formula and sterilizing baby bottles, and get ready to cook dinner.

Then it happened ... I remember that fateful day as if it were yesterday. All of a sudden the lights went out; the electricity was off. My husband and I earned a considerable combined income—more than enough to pay the bills. Accordingly, my first reaction was to check to see if the rest of the block was out. Well, everybody else had lights, so you know the deal ...my husband had not paid the bill, and the electric company shut off the power.

To this day, I don't know why or what happened. Did he simply forget? Did he spend the money? I didn't care. My marriage was already stressed. I was already flying around like Superwoman trying to do everything with little-to-no help from my husband. All he had to do was pay the bill. How was I supposed to take care of everything that needed to be done with no lights?

I looked at my husband, and my face must have appeared to be splitting into parts with sparks and smoke shooting out because, although I hadn't said a word he started grabbing babies, milk, and baby bags. He took us over to the house of some friends, Steve and Charlotte. I was able to get the babies settled, and they fixed us dinner.

Later that night I was talking to Steve and feeling pretty low. It seemed that, no matter how hard I tried to be the best wife and mother, my life was crashing down all around me, and no one could explain to me why my American dream was turning into the American nightmare. Why? I am a good person; I am doing everything that is asked of me. Then why isn't the plan working? Sitting there that night with Steve, I shared my pain—pain that I usually kept hidden from the world.

During our conversation I said to him, "My mother used to always say that if you did something wrong, it would come back to you, or possibly down your family line to your children. Well, my ancestors must have been tearing their butts, because I'm catching hell."

Steve said, "No, it's not what somebody else did; it's what you did in a previous life."

I said, "What? Me? In a previous life?"

Steve could tell by my reaction that I knew little to nothing about reincarnation. He disappeared into the back room, returning with a book, *Life After Life* by Raymond Moody Jr. This was my introduction to reincarnation, and the rest is history.

Talk about an "aha" moment! Reading that book was like traveling through a wormhole to another existence. A whole new world of possibilities opened up for me. My old belief system, now full of holes, was rapidly disappearing as a new system of beliefs began taking me to new heights of understanding.

As I read the book, I came to understand that when you "die," the body returns to the earth but your essence—your memories and experiences "live" on. In addition, all of your deeds are recorded in an invisible book called the Akashic Records. And some time in the distant future, when it's your time to return to the Earth, you have the opportunity to balance your record of deeds. You have lessons to learn, so to speak.

I cannot begin to tell you how my life changed after reading that book. I realized I was in a box wrapped in belief systems and "-isms" that kept me bound and held victim. As long as I believed that what someone else had done caused my pain or that someone else was responsible for my pain, I had no control. When I realized that I am responsible for my life, I realized that I have the control. The responsibility to stand up and take action to change my situation is *my* choice. Subsequently, my sojourn into the metaphysical world gained in velocity; I read everything I could get my hands on to increase my knowledge.

Once you step out of your comfort zone and open yourself to new horizons, the universe will flood you with new information. Again, there is something to be said about the phrase, "Seek and ye shall find." With that said, as I continued to study, I found there was some truth to my mother's saying about passing on your deeds (or misdeeds) down to your children. But we will touch on that later.

As I began to evolve in my understandings, my life changed, and I changed. And, yes, part of my growth required that I take my sons and move on to experience life at a different level.

This was just one more experience leading me on the spiritual path, discovering my power within. I don't have to be a second-class citizen; I can be a free citizen of the universe. But I still had a long way to go and lots of lessons to learn. My "aha" moments leading to spiritual transformation were just beginning.

Tapping the Power

The more I learned the more I understood and the more it all came together, resulting in my realization that there is only the One—the Oneness of it All. And the All is Energy. The more I understood, the more I realized that I have the Power! The Power is within me! I create my own reality. I am, in fact, co-creator of the universe.

My introduction to Eastern philosophy spurred my initial awareness of the concept that there is only One, and to access the power you must look within. Intrigued by this new information, I continued to research and amass knowledge of metaphysical concepts. However, there is a major difference between acquiring knowledge and practicing that which you have learned. It was not until I read Iyanla Vanzant's book, *Tapping the Power Within*, that I embarked upon an actual spiritual "practice." Reading Iyanla's book presented lots of "aha" moments and was truly a life-changing experience.

After reading her book, I set up my first altar of sacred space and began to practice meditation. Consequently, it was Iyanla who taught me *how* to access the power within. Iyanla, I thank you!

To make the point, all of the metaphysical information brought a more profound comprehension of the adage, "Know Thyself."

This inspires knowledge of self from a spiritual/universal realm. Aha! The more profound my understanding of energy, the more power I realized I had, which resulted in FREEDOM. I witnessed a change in my thinking and a change in my behavior.

No one has control over me. If I find myself in a situation that I don't like, then it's up to me to change it. I went from being a victim to being a victor. I went from feeling pain to a sense of peace. I went from blaming others to taking responsibility. I went from anger to forgiveness. I went from feeling controlled to being in control; I went from being powerless to being powerful.

I can't tell you how empowering freedom feels. I now conduct my life operating from a whole new perspective, with a new set of laws in my life. And that is what led me to write this story and share what I learned with you.

Well, there you have the story of my rocky beginnings. Now it's time to move on and really do some deep diving and identify the anchors that weigh us down.

RECOGNIZE the Anchors of Limitation

Chapter 2

Anchors of Limitation

Okay, now that you've heard my story as I shared some of my "aha" moments that created pivotal turning points in my life, it is time for you to do some self-reflection. It's time for you to do some deep diving into the depths of your soul and discover what's weighing you down.

What are the anchors weighing you down and preventing you from setting sail to your desired destination? This represents the "drydock" where the vessel is stuck.

There is a massive anchor hidden deep within the dark waters. We can't see it, but it has a firm grip on our vessel, preventing any motion forward. Before we can get underway, we must find the anchor. Before we can accomplish anything in life, we must identify the anchor(s). It is such a critical phase in the process.

In order to take control of your life, you must *Recognize* the *Anchors of Limitation*—limitations brought on by fears, belief systems, and life experiences. We will discuss the process of releasing the anchors in a later chapter. Right now we've got our hands full just finding the anchors.

Identify Your Belief Systems

What are the limiting beliefs that keep you from being the best you can be?

Is it fear of success, fear of death, or fear of what someone else will say?

Is it one of the "-isms" telling you that you are not good enough: racism, sexism, or ageism?

Or is it one of the following institutions?

- Religion – telling you to wait for your reward in heaven, or that God is a vengeful and jealous God.
- Education – telling you someone else's "his-story" or teaching you scientific theories that don't hold water.

This book contains the secrets to identifying the anchors of limitation, so you may experience transformation and true freedom.

Defining Power

In order to take control of one's life, one must first ask: Who is in control now? Are you, or is someone else at the helm? Well, what does control really look like? Does being in control of your life mean that you have all of the necessities of life and maybe a few luxuries?

You've got the spouse, the house, two kids, the dog, and life is good. Your family life is good; your spiritual life appears to be on track; and you are in good standing in the community. All in all, your life seems to be pretty successful. Does this equate with being in control? Let's look at the word *control*.

Control means to have power over, or to be in power, and empowered means to be without limitation. If you are bound by limitations, then you are not really free. If you are not free, then are you really in control?

It is my contention that African Americans are not yet free. Better yet, I say that humanity is not free; we have all been imprisoned in "Boxes" in one form or another. Humanity remains in bondage, whether we know it or not.

Except for the few who have learned TRUTH from the ancient ones, humanity exists in a mental bondage, an illusionary world. We as humans live in a box of systems—value systems, belief systems, institutions, and all the "-isms"—all dictating societal norms that we must abide by if we are to be perceived as "good" persons or citizens. This box becomes a prison for your mind, as was so eloquently stated by Morpheus in the movie *The Matrix*.

Analyze Your Anchors

Your earthly socialization begins shortly after birth when that doctor smacks you on your butt. Yes, you are in control for a little while. Although you start out dependent on others for food and shelter, you piss and poop at will and cry when you want attention.

At first you have your parents at your beck-and-call. Then, slowly, this arrangement begins to shift as your parents begin to condition you to the "timetable." The older you get the more conditioning; breakfast at eight, lunch at twelve, dinner at six. As you grow older, you continue to conform to societal rules and next thing you know, it's bed by ten, up by seven, breakfast at eight, off to work by nine, lunch at twelve, home by five, dinner at six, and the routine starts all over again.

The socializing begins at birth and continues on into later life as we learn how to behave in the system(s) from:
- Our parents, as they teach us to believe the belief system as it was taught to them by their parents;

- Institutions instilling the norms, beliefs, rules and regulations of the institution of education and/or the institution of religion
- All the systems – political system, the system of white supremacy, and so on
- All the "-isms" such as
  - Racism – a belief that one race is superior to another and seeks to maintain control of the latter based on that belief system
  - Sexism – setting the standard of behavior for a particular gender, such as what jobs one may or may not apply for
  - Age-ism – determining if one is too old or too young to work

Once we recognize and comprehend that there is a system that has us mentally imprisoned, only then can we discern the affects created by the "Boxes."

How the Anchors Show Up in Life

Enclosed in various "Boxes" —full of values, beliefs, the norms, and standards, as well as the rules and regulations—our minds remain captive. Told how to behave, what is good, what is bad, how we should look, think, act, etc., we conform to the system with little to no question.

How does this show up in our daily lives? As long as we stay in the box of acceptable behavior, everything is fine. The moment we dare to step out of the box, our behavior is perceived as unacceptable. We are considered troublemakers or non-conformists, and may possibly be subjected to repercussions from society. As a result, we react with feelings of shame and guilt.

Thus, we are afraid to step out of the box. We are afraid to challenge the system, afraid to ask the questions, you know…the questions we are afraid to ask for fear someone might think we're stupid or crazy…afraid to rock the boat or box, as it were. Or, if we are brave enough to ask the questions, the answers are not to our satisfaction.

Perhaps this response sounds all too familiar: "There are just some things we are not supposed to know" or "You'll get your answers in heaven."

Consequently, we go through life following the system according to someone else's design of how we should act, think, feel, and so on. When we conform to the system, then we are no longer in control.

The next thing we know we are no longer living for ourselves; we are living according to someone else's standards. We have completely lost our autonomy, our control, and our freedom.

As we blindly follow along with the systems and relinquish control, we have now become victims, living our lives with someone else directing our course.

Humanity at large is steeped in this victim mentality, and we humans routinely shift the blame for what ails us onto someone else.

Even as a young child, we search for someone to blame. As an illustration, we've all seen the little one who trips and falls. When asked what happened, she points to the first person she sees and says, "He did it…he pushed me!"

Victim mentality—where does it come from? It begins with losing control of our lives. We can only be a victim if we have given control of our life to someone else. Thus, a victim is one who is subjected to oppression, or one who is acted upon. So when we relinquish control of our mind and our thoughts, we unwittingly and voluntarily give someone else access to our mind, body, and soul. If things go well, we can feel good about life now that we have given someone else the responsibility for our life. If things go badly, now we have someone to blame.

Either we are victims with no control, or we are victors and in control of our life's destination.

And humanity will maintain in victim mentality until we step out of the comfort zone, ask the questions, and learn that there is more to life than meets the eye.

In addition to the box humanity is encased in, African Americans appear to have some super-duper, doubled-sided, steel-laden boxes. It's as if we need a sandblaster to drill through them all.

With the advent of white supremacy and slavery, we suffered a deeper form of mind imprisonment. It is one thing to voluntarily accept the systems and conform. By contrast, it is quite another to be forced into a system and have the system forcefully ingrained deep within your very being. This relates back to the concept of African Americans suffering from psychic trauma. The physical chains have been removed, but the mental and spiritual chains still have quite a grip on our soul. Thus, we as African Americans tend to be more reluctant to step out of the box.

With all of that said, now we must figure out how to reclaim our freedom—true freedom. We have to claim it on two levels: a cultural freedom, learning who we are as African Americans, and a spiritual freedom, learning that we are citizens of the universe.

What's holding you back?

How do you regain control of your life?

Freedom to Succeed

So where does the journey begin to take control, to gain access to freedom of our mind, body, and soul? We have got to recognize that we are bound by limiting belief systems. Limiting thoughts from all the institutions, bound by the chains of the "-isms." Bound by feelings of fear, doubt, guilt, and shame afraid to rock the boat or box, as it were—all anchors weighing us down and holding us back.

Navigate Your Existence!

Subsequently, we must identify the anchors of limitation weighing us down and release them so we may rise.

We must break the chains of limiting beliefs, the information fed to us through the institutions, and break free from all the "-isms." We need to release old belief systems that are not serving us anymore and make way for new ideas and beliefs (although there is nothing new under the sun).

Only by discovering the anchors that enclose us in the boxes can we begin the process of breaking out. We all exist in the boxes—many different ones all at once. You know, like the Russia dolls; you open one and inside there is another smaller doll and you continue until finally there are no more dolls. The "Boxes" are similar to the layers of Russia dolls. You have to keep breaking out until there are no more boxes and you are free.

My story began with a big box of white supremacy that showed up in my life through racism, affected my educational process, fed into my religious beliefs, and continued influencing my life. Each of you will have to travel your own road in identifying your anchors and breaking through those limiting belief systems on your journey to freedom.

Discovering your anchors is a process in and of itself. Releasing the anchors is also a process requiring the acquisition of information. It demands a certain amount of know-how. How do you release that anchor? Do you yank it out of the water? Do you wiggle it? Are there tools that can assist in making your task easier?

So before we can release the anchors, there is quite a bit of ground to cover. Then and only then will we know how to release the anchors properly.

As we progress on my journey of "aha" moments, the secrets will continue to unfold and reveal the knowledge and the tools necessary for you to break out of the boxes and take control of your life and find true liberation. When your mind is free, no one can truly possess you. Or, like that saying goes, "Free your mind and your butt will follow."

CATCH THE WAVE – *Chapter Summary*

IMPORTANT POINTS TO REMEMBER

- Humanity suffers from victim mentality existing in a mental bondage—an illusionary world.
- Our minds are enclosed in "Boxes" full of values, beliefs, norms, and standards, as well as rules and regulations.
- We are told how to behave, what is good, what is bad, how we should look, think, and act. Stepping out of the "Box," or realm of expected behavior, may bring about repercussions.
- Socialization begins at birth as we develop our belief systems from our parents, institutions, and all the "-isms."
- As we accept these belief systems and incorporate them into our lives, we relinquish control of our thoughts, thus becoming victims.
- In order to gain control and move from victim to victor, one must acquire knowledge, realize the powers within, and release the *anchors of limitation*.
  - For African Americans, all of the aforementioned statements are true. However, our socialization consisted of an involuntary *construct* forced upon us and solidified through violence. It creates a deeper reluctance to buck the system or step out of the "Box."

ACTION STEPS

Identifying the *anchors of limitation* in your life is a process. Begin this action step by jotting down answers that come to mind easily and quickly. As you proceed along our journey, you will uncover fears and limiting beliefs that are buried deep within. Ultimately, you may revisit this task a few times, adding a little more each trip.

- Identify your fears and limiting beliefs
  - Write a list of FEARS. What are you afraid of?
  - List any limiting beliefs you may have and how it has affected your life. Identify where you acquired these limiting beliefs. Did they come from:
    - Parents?
    - Family?
    - Work?
    - School?
    - Church?

LIFE LESSONS FOR TRANSFORMATION

Recognizing your limitations is such a critical step in your transformation. You must identify what's weighing you down or holding you back. Again, you can't begin to solve the problem if you don't know what the problem is.

One of my greatest fears in life was the fear of fire. I first learned of my fear when, while traveling home from college, the car started smoking. At the time I didn't know much about cars, but I knew that smoke coming from under the hood was not a good thing. For me, all I could think of was "Where there's smoke, there's fire," and I wanted out of that car.

Preparing to stop the car, my friend pulled off the highway. Not waiting for the car to stop, I jumped out of the car and ran to distance myself from any possible danger. Standing there on the side of the road, far away from the car is when I realized my fear of fire. Yet, I had no idea where the fear originated from or what caused my fear.

Moreover, I lived with that fear well into my adult life. It was not until I attended a conference and was forced to do some soul-searching that I figured out the exact moment the fear of fire became a part of my life.

One of the tenets at the conference was, when given the correct knowledge, you can accomplish anything. To solidify the message, each participant was expected to "eat fire" like the fire-eaters at the circus. Excuse me? I was not about to put a burning rod anywhere near my mouth. While I was sitting there waiting my turn to "eat fire," I engaged in some deep reflection. Where did my fear of fire come from? As I was tracing my life backward, it hit me. It was that day—the day the incinerator blew up in the hallway.

Living in the projects, we had trash incinerators in the hallway right by the elevators. There was no need to take your trash down to the curb. However, there was a warning posted cautioning against placing loose particles into the incinerator. My eleven-year-old neighbor dropped a bag of flour, swept it up, put it in the trash, and attempted to empty the bag into the incinerator.

Immediately, it caused an explosion that sent a loud boom around the hall, banging on each door as the energy from the explosion tried to escape enclosure. I remember running to the door. When I opened it, all I saw was my neighbor running down the hall screaming, her arms stretched out with trails of fire streaming from each limb. I can still see it like it was yesterday. There…that was it. I finally figured out the incident that caused my fear of fire. Although badly burned, my neighbor survived the trauma and went on with her life. However, I had no idea the effect the incident had on me—that I—too, was traumatized.

So back to the conference, there I sat listening intently as the process to safely "eat fire" was explained. The conference presenters assured us that if we followed instructions, we would not get burned.

I watched as person after person placed the fiery rod in their mouths with no issue. Now usually, I'm a risk-taker and up for any challenge. But fire…now that's another story.

However, armed with my newly-acquired knowledge, I was ready to go for it. Ready, set, go…and I did it! I ate the fire! And that was the end of my lifelong fear of fire. *Anchors of limitation*! My fear of fire caused me stress and strife on a number of occasions in my life. And just like that, through acquiring the proper knowledge, I was able to release my fear. There is a saying…FEAR is False Evidence Appearing Real. This is such a perfect example.

Hopefully, my experience gives you major insight as to how critical identifying your anchors is to your evolution. Knowing your limitation is the first part of the puzzle. As we progress through this journey, you will acquire knowledge to shift your thoughts and habits, allowing you to release old baggage and fears brought on by the systems, "-isms," institutions, or prior life experiences. We'll discuss more about releasing the anchors later. But first, we need to progress to our next Key to the African American Resurrection.

RESTORE the Knowledge of the Ancestors

Chapter 3

Time Waits for No One

What Time Is It??

As we continue to Chart the Course—gathering knowledge and information for our journey—it is important that we assess the time. Prior to setting sail or "Getting Underway," collecting information regarding the timing of your voyage is critical.

What time of year is it, what season is it, and how will this affect your trip? Are the waters going to be smooth or choppy, and might they become turbulent? Will you encounter dangerous weather or run into glaciers along your route? Will the seasons change during the course of your journey? And what about the stars and constellations? How will the timing of your journey play into the shifting celestial bodies in the skies?

When you think about it, the element of time plays an integral part in the planning of your journey. So, what time is it?

Let's take a moment to look at the times we currently find ourselves in. I don't think anyone would argue the point that the times, "they-are-a-changing." In times past, people would make the statement, "It seems like time is speeding up," or "Time sure is flying by." Now people are acknowledging that time *is* moving faster. They are not sure why or how it's happening, but there is no shortage of people who believe the concept to be true.

Are you finding it harder to get things accomplished in an eight-hour day? Do you find yourself wishing for more hours so you might complete that list of "things to do?" Are you among the multitudes of people absolutely astonished that it seems like it was just New Year's and now the year is almost over? Would you like to know what's really going on? Well, hang in there with me as we pick up speed.

2012 and Beyond

The following information discusses great changes on Earth and in the skies that occurred on December 21, 2012. The changes have already begun and the effects will last for quite some time after the date.

Many people equate the "times" with the biblical battle of Armageddon and "End of the World" prophecies. We've always heard of the coming of Armageddon, and many anticipate its arrival with great apprehension. In recent years there has been an increasing buzz that the exact date designated for the end of the world, Armageddon, was December 21, 2012.

Actually, it's not the first time a date had been assigned for the end of the world "doomsday theories." Many of us recall the ringing in of the New Millennium on December 31, 1999, which was the last time designated for "it all to end." I have no doubt that, over the years, there have been numerous times and dates signifying the end of the world, and yet here we are.

So what do we know about the impact of December 21, 2012? Let's explore its origins, what most people acknowledge about this date, and what other information has been circulated regarding it.

Navigate Your Existence!

Let's begin with what's considered common knowledge about the date. Many people are aware that the winter solstice occurs on or around December 21. The winter solstice also marks the celebration of Christmas, which means the date designated for the celebration— December 25— has a connection to astrology. The winter solstice is when the Earth's axis is facing farthest from the sun, resulting in the longest night of the year. It happens annually like clockwork. So, then, what is so significant about the year 2012?

THE WINTER SOLSTICE

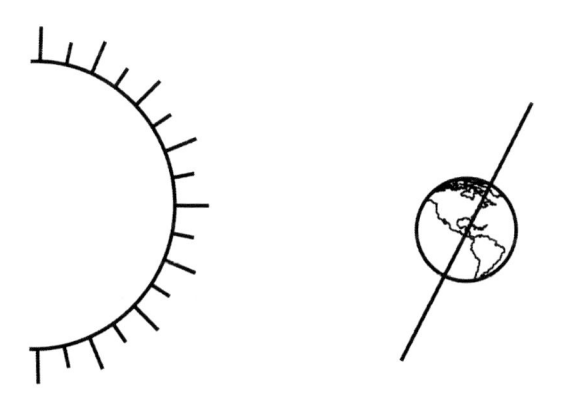

The winter solstice occurs as the Earth's axis is facing farthest from the sun, resulting in the longest night of the year.

That brings us to the topic of the Mayan Calendar. Until recently, there was not a lot of discussion about the calendar, but lately it seems to have become a hot topic.

The Mayan Calendar is but one of many ancient calendars that have been recording time for thousands of years by charting the movement of celestial bodies in the sky and forecasting events affecting the Earth and humanity. This astronomical information was liter-

THE MAYAN CALENDAR

The Mayan Calendar we hear so much about is the fourth
of many Mayan calendars called the Tzolk'in or Cholq'ij.
It is extremely detailed in its depictions of dates and events in time.

ally etched into stone by many of the indigenous people in many parts of the world, such as the Kemites/Egyptians, Mayans, Q'ero elders of Peru, the Navajo, Cherokee, and Dogons, just to name a few. Actually, the Mayans received their astrological heritage from their predecessors, the Olmecs.

At any rate, the Mayan Calendar we hear so much about is the fourth of many Mayan calendars called the *Tzolk'in* or *Cholq'ij*. It is extremely detailed in its depictions of dates and events in time. Much of the discussion rallies around the issue that the calendar, which has recorded time and events for hundreds of thousands of years, simply stopped on December 21, 2012. This has led many to the conclusion that the Mayans were predicting the end of the world. The "End of the World" prophecies are called "The End of Creation," "Judgment Day," "Armageddon," "The Time of Great Purification," "The End of Time As We Know it," and other descriptions, according to various cultural traditions.

What time is it?

In order to understand the Mayan Calendar and its implications of time and relevance to humanity, we must first understand that many of the calendars are based on calculated *periods* of time called *cycles*, *ages*, or *worlds*. These terms are used interchangeably since they all signify a period of time. These various great cycles in the universe speak of great events: The Great Zodiac Cycle, The Great Galactic Alignment, The Five Worlds, and The Zodiac Cycle. All of these cycles are based on astrology.

> *"Astrology is the study of how events on earth correspond to the positions and movements of astronomical bodies. These astronomical bodies included are the sun, moon, planets, and stars depending on the position of their bodies at the exact time of a person's birth; astrologers believe the bodies and their movements reflect that person's character. The*

knowledge of the person's character and their [sic] relation to the bodies enables astrologers to predict a person's destiny. This prediction is not limited to one person. A prediction could be for an individual, group, or nation."
– **Nicki Tesch, astrologer**

With regard to astrology, we must pay tribute to the first calendar to chart the skies. The Mandela in Dendera, Egypt, is known as the original map of the sky. The Kemites/Egyptians charted the skies and constructed the Mandela in Pre-Dynastic Kemet/Egypt. It is from this ancient calendar that the signs of the zodiac emerged as well as other calendars that charted the times astronomically. As the history of man's relationship with astrology unfolds, it assists us in understanding the significance of the Mayan calendar.

THE MANDALA OF DENDERA
The Kemetic/Egyptian Astrological Calendar

The Mandela of Dendera – *The Kemetic/Egyptian Astrological Calendar* is known as the original map of the sky. The Kemites/Egyptians charted the skies and constructed the Mandela in Pre-Dynastic Kemet/Egypt. It is from this ancient calendar that the signs of the zodiac emerged as well as other calendars that charted the times astronomically.

Let's take a look at the cycles forecast by the Mayan calendar and their implications for the Earth and humanity.

Okay, right about now you might want to grab on to something as we head into high seas and rough waters. We're about to cover a lot of information, but hold on. As we progress along our journey, it will all become clear why this information is so important to you as you Navigate Your Existence.

THE GREAT ZODIAC CYCLE

It takes approximately 26,000 years for the Earth to rotate through all twelve zodiac signs.
12 X 2,160 = 25,920 or (approx. 26,000 years)

The Great Zodiac Cycle

The Great Zodiac is a band across the sky divided into twelve parts, or signs named after the constellations. The Great Zodiac Cycle extends over an approximate 26,000-year period. This is the time it takes our planet's equatorial plane, due to the wobble of its axis, to complete a cycle along the solar ecliptic.

In other words, it's the time it takes our planet to travel one full rotation along the path of the sun through each of the twelve constellations or zodiac signs. This 26,000-year cycle also rotates every 12,000 years between a cycle of ascension of consciousness, in which humanity is very aware, and a 12,000-year cycle of "descension," in which humanity experiences a decrease in consciousness, or a sleep cycle, and is not as aware.

It is very similar to what we experience every twenty-four-hour period on Earth. We spend half of our day awake, and the other half in a sleep state. The conceptualization of a 26,000-year cycle can be a bit difficult, given the fact that the human life span is less than one hundred years. And let's not forget that many were led to believe (and some still do) that civilization only began around 5,000 to 3,000 B.C.

There is yet another quite remarkable event that occurs only once every 26,000 years called the Great Galactic Alignment. And, yes, this event occurred during the winter solstice on December 21, 2012. With the Earth's axis titled farthest away from the sun, it aligned perfectly with the center of our galaxy. The center of the Milky Way and the axis of the Earth coordinated in what is called the Great Galactic Alignment. Accordingly, some say that the alignment ushered in cosmic energy to increase the vibration of the Earth—in a sense, a speeding up of sorts. So, yes, time is speeding up. This energy will increase and intensify the changes due to be experienced by Earth and all of her inhabitants. Simply amazing!

THE GREAT GALACTIC ALIGNMENT

Our Galaxy The Milky Way ←

← Earth

On December 21, 2012 the Earth's axis aligned perfectly with the center of our galaxy – The Milky Way. This event only occurs once every 26,000 years.

The Five "Worlds" or "Suns"

The Great Zodiac cycle of 26,000 years is also divided into five smaller cycles or "worlds." Each "world" or time period lasts approximately 5,125 years. The five "worlds" do not necessarily correspond with astrological cycles, but the end of this fourth world does. The fourth world began in 3113 B.C. and was scheduled to end in 2012 A.D. The Mayans referred to these "worlds" as "suns." So, it would be said that we're leaving the fourth "sun" and entering the fifth.

There seems to be some disagreement regarding whether we've entered the fifth or sixth period; however, most agree on the events that will occur and/or the effects experienced by Earth and humanity.

Each "sun" or period is said to be governed by one of the elements: fire, earth, air, and water. Unbeknownst to many, it is also said that each 5,125 year period the Earth was "destroyed" by one of the elements. To bring some relevancy to this concept, think about the biblical story of Noah and the flood. Remember that in this last period, the Earth was "destroyed" by water.

It seems that every 5,000 years or so, the Earth transitions through major changes and one of the elements plays a significant part. Usually, when speaking of the elements, we discuss what are known as the terrestrial elements: earth, wind, fire, and water. However, there is a fifth element; ether. According to Webster's New Collegiate Dictionary, ether is "1.a.: the rarefied element formerly believed to fill the upper regions of space; b: the upper regions of space, heavens; 2.a.: a medium that in the wave theory of light permeates all space and transmits transverse waves."

Okay, now let me translate that into plain English. Ether is thought of as the "space" that fills the heavens. And although we don't pay much attention to ether, it is actually the space that fills even the earthly elements of earth, water, fire, and air. Some consider it the spiritual energy that permeates all that exists in the universe.

Now that's getting a little deep. We'll touch on ether again further on in the journey and you will come to understand why this information is important as you Chart the Course for your own life.

But for now what's important to know is that as we enter the Fifth Sun, it will be the element of ether that will reign supreme. Ether, that spiritual energy that permeates all, will become more prevalent in our lives. It will be *ether* that affects the changes in our bodies, our environment, and our very existence.

THE ZODIAC CYCLES

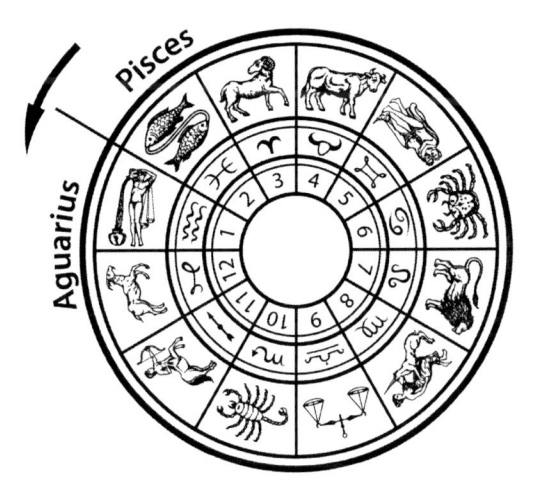

A Zodiac Cycle is just one of the twelve Zodiac Cycles or signs. Each of the twelve zodiac signs lasts an average of 2,160 years. Earth is transitioning from the Zodiac Cycle of Pisces to the Zodiac Cycle of Aquarius.

The Zodiac Cycle

With regard to time, the Zodiac Cycle is another important tool for navigating your existence. A Zodiac Cycle (just one sign) is but one-twelfth of the Great Zodiac Cycle (all twelve signs). It represents the period the Earth is in just one constellation or zodiac sign. The zodiac cycles vary in lengths of time and can last anywhere between 2,000 to 2,300 years. The average for each of the twelve signs is approximately 2,160 years, times twelve, which equals 25,920 (or about 26,000 years).

Currently, our planet is just leaving the zodiac sign of Pisces, one of the short ages. Each "age" has a theme. Individuals, groups, and nations have characteristics based on astrology, and so do planets. Although the theme for Pisces is "spiritual," it sits in the eighth house of Libra, which represents death.

Therefore, the age of Pisces ushered in a 2,000-year period of death, deceit, destruction, and continued in the 12,000-year "descension" in consciousness (or decrease in awareness or sleep). The age of Pisces is not a good cycle for our planet.

Earth is just transitioning from the Age of Pisces into the Age of Aquarius. The theme of the Age of Aquarius is enlightenment, thus, it is also known as the Age of Enlightenment. The exact date that the Age of Aquarius is due to begin is a matter of great debate. Many people believe that Pisces began with the birth of Christ in 1 A.D. and would end approximately in the year 2000 or (2012), ringing in the Age of Aquarius.

Some calculations chart the beginning of Pisces as late as 498 B.C., which would place the beginning of the Age of Aquarius at approximately 2658 A.D. The most common calculations that I've found place Pisces beginning between 60 B.C. and 26 A.D., and the Age of Aquarius beginning between 1997 and 2160 A.D.

As we near the end of an age or draw close to the beginning of another, the effects of the new age become more apparent. It is called "being on the cusp" (or verge) of the next age since the energies of both signs can be felt. It can take hundreds of years before Earth completely shifts into the next zodiac sign in the pattern of the Great Zodiac Cycle. With each age lasting an average of 2,160 years, I don't think the variation of one hundred years or so in the calculations of the ages is extremely significant. We are already experiencing the effects of the Age of Aquarius. With so many cycles having ended and started on December 12, 2012, I tend to agree that this was the actual beginning of the Age of Aquarius.

In contrast to the age of Pisces, the Age of Aquarius/Age of Enlightenment is considered to be good for our planet. One of the reasons for this is because, during the Age of Aquarius, our planet will enter into the Photon Belt.

Okay, now what is a Photon Belt and what does it have to do with your journey? Stay with me here and just digest this; it will all make sense as your voyage unfolds.

Simply stated, a photon is a unit of light. The Photon Belt is a band of intense photon/light energy that the Earth is set to be affected by for the next 2,000 years. And, yes, as of December 21, 2012, the Earth became fully positioned in the midst of the belt.

The changes we hear about with regard to the Age of Aquarius begin with the effects of this enormous influx of energy from the Photon Belt. This great influx of cosmic energy will cause the vibration of the Earth to heighten and affect all upon it. The increase in vibration is another reason we feel a sense of time speeding up. There will be a shift in consciousness, an increase in awareness. It will be a time to reconnect with Divine Energy.

Earth moving into the Photon Belt will also create massive changes in the weather and upheavals on the planet. The transition through this period can be easy or it can be hard. How each of us fares during these changes will depend on whether or not we are ready. It will depend largely on the state of our consciousness. In the Age of Aquarius, one will be expected to demonstrate unconditional love and forgiveness, live in peace with others, respect all life, and respect Mother Earth and nature.

Wow! Talk about changes. As we come to understand the predictions of the Mayan Calendar and how the ancients used the terms "worlds," "ages," and "cycles," it affords us an opportunity to transform our perception of the End-of-the-World prophesies. We can entertain the concept that it is not the end of the world, but the end of a "World Era." Yes, the world is going to end as we know it, for the changes we will experience will be remarkable. Interestingly enough, some people are already feeling the energy surges, but others may not. However, know that the influx of energy continues to increase.

Right about now, someone out there is saying, "That's a lot of good information, but what does it have to do with me?" Okay, so you're sailing in the middle of the ocean and you begin to notice the waters changing. The waves are growing in intensity. You can't see it, but you sense a wave of immense power headed your way. What do you do?

Should you do nothing and follow along your same course as if nothing is changing? Or do you prepare for the inevitable. Do you change your course of action? Does it matter if it is a wave of water or a wave of energy? A wave is coming…the Earth is changing…our world is ending as we know it. You have a choice as to how well you transition these times. Either continue on your course and take the wave head-on, or rise in consciousness and go with the flow.

Astrology: Real or Fantasy?

Okay, now I know that whirlwind of information was probably new to many of you. As we continue, other concepts will build on one another and help make sense of it all, so hang in there with me. It's really a fantastic ride! And, again, when we are introduced to new concepts, it takes courage to step away from what is comfortable…to step outside of your comfort zone.

Now, remember, I'm not here to challenge anyone's belief system—we're just taking a look at things from a different perspective. All of the aforementioned discussions of events in time are based on astrology.

Do you recall the song, "Age of Aquarius" and the words… *"This is the dawning of the Age of Aquarius?"* It's such a popular song, and I'm sure most of you have heard it at some point. I don't particularly want to date myself, but I recall when the song was on the top hit list. Everyone was singing it. We knew it had something to do with astrology, but back in the '60s not many people in the mainstream were studying astrology.

As a matter of fact, many religious groups declared that astrology was in the realm of metaphysics (the unseen) and therefore was considered "of the devil." Having grown up in a traditional Baptist Church with a Black congregation, we were forbidden to talk about astrology or, heaven forbid, even read or research the topic. Believe it or not, at one point, I was actually afraid to touch a book on astrology. It was thought to be the "occult," which many still equate with witchcraft. Occult means "hidden, secret, mysterious, or of the mystic arts." Astrology was thought of as the "occult" because many didn't understand the concept of unseen forces in the universe.

For those who still don't believe in astrology or that the celestial bodies have an effect on our bodies, please allow me to take a moment and share an experience I had with someone who associated astrology with dark or evil forces. It may serve to provide a frame of reference and/or a level of comfort to some who still connect astrology to negative forces. In addition, it may also help someone overcome the fear of astrology and take that first step to begin researching the subject with an open mind.

I was in the teachers' lounge explaining my sun sign of Scorpio to my good friend, both of us second-grade teachers, when another teacher, Betty, overheard the conversation. "You shouldn't be talking about that stuff," she said. "It's of the devil." I called her over and asked, "Betty, don't we teach the cycles of the moon in the second-grade curriculum every year?" She replied, "Yes, of course." "Well, would you agree that the oceans, which constitute three-fourths of the planet, are affected by the gravitational pull of the moon every day as the tide pulls the waters out to sea every morning and returns them to the shores every evening?" I asked. "Yes," she agreed. I proceeded to explain that, just like the Earth, our bodies are also three-fourths water. I then asked her if she thought it possible for the moon to have an effect on the water in our bodies as well. She had to think about it for a moment, but then she said, "Yes, that makes sense."

Well, Betty, that's basically all astrology is! It is the effect the sun, moon, stars, or celestial bodies in the sky have on our bodies. It is science—an exact science. There is nothing spooky or devilish about it. Astrology is just misunderstood and still suffers from negative connotations.

To further drive the point home, let me share another aspect of my relationship with Betty. She and I taught across the hall from each other for years and enjoyed our relationship as peers. However, outwardly, Betty and I appeared to be as different as day and night.

Betty was most likely reared in the Midwest, in a small rural town. She was White with a head full of red hair. Then there was me: reared in Harlem, the Mecca of the Black Cultural Revolution. At that time, I wore my hair in a short, natural or Afro style with big earrings. Coming from two vastly different cultural upbringings, the only thing we had in common, so we thought, was that we were both excellent second-grade teachers.

One day we discovered that we not only shared the same sun sign of Scorpio, but that we were also born on the same day. It is a rare occurrence to find someone in your circle of acquaintances who has the same birthday. Now I was never really a "morning" person. It was well known by the staff not to bother me on Monday morning till I woke up. Around noon, I'd be much more open to hearing that story you wanted to tell me. Well, Betty was the exact same way. After realizing that we shared the same sun sign, we began to pay close attention and discovered many other similarities in our personalities.

Astrology is an intricate and profound science, and astrologers study astronomy, or the celestial bodies, in detail. Actually, at one time there was no differentiation made between the study of astronomy and astrology. If one truly understood astronomy, it was accepted that celestial bodies have an effect on humans, groups, and planets, which represents the astrological aspect of astronomy.

Currently, many people deal with astrology as more of a hobby versus studying it on a deeper, more scientific level. In general, most of the discussions commonly heard about astrology have to do with an individual's sun sign, or just one of the twelve zodiac signs.

The position of the celestial bodies, (planets and stars) when you were born determines your sun sign and plays a role in determining your basic characteristics. The discussion of one's sun sign just scratches the surface of the profound information available when one gets serious about the science of astrology.

Hopefully, my experiences with astrology helped to provide a better understanding of the effects the celestial bodies have on individuals and planets. And hopefully, this will help you to bring some perspective to WHAT IN THE WORLD IS GOING ON? or What Time Is It?

Further along in our voyage, you'll understand why. But let's wrap this up with one more important concept as you Chart the Course.

The Age of Aquarius

Some say these are scary times. Many people are truly frightened and afraid of the prophesied "End of the World."

Yes, we are witnessing horrific natural disasters just as was forecast, including plagues, pestilence, and upheavals in the Earth.

In October 2012, people experienced the wrath of "Superstorm Sandy" that hit the Atlantic coast with a vengeance. Superstorm Sandy claimed the lives of 253 persons and caused $65 billion in damage. There was no need to wait for Dec 21, 2012 for the world to end; it was ending "as we know it" right before our very eyes.

Yet with the end of a "World," there is the beginning of a new "World."

We are at the end of Pisces and the beginning of the Age of Aquarius: the end of a 26,000-year period and the beginning of another 26,000-year period.

The end of a 12,000-year period of "descension" (decline in consciousness) and the beginning of a 12,000-year period of ascension, (increase in consciousness); the end of a 5,125-year *world*, and the beginning of a new 5,125-year *world*; and a Great Galactic Alignment that hasn't occurred for 26,000 years.

Are these scary times? I say these are exciting times! It all depends on whether you and your ship are in order. What time is it? It is time to raise your consciousness and actively prepare for the Beginning of the New World.

Discovering this knowledge freed me from the doom-and-gloom mentality in which so many people live. I no longer have to go through life fearful of the future. Fear causes anxiety. The human body, your ship, cannot perform optimally from a position of fear.

Will I experience one of Earth's catastrophes? Who knows, but at least I now understand why the Earth is experiencing these events. How will *you* navigate through these extraordinary times? What time is it? It is time to gather the necessary information and prepare to be the conductor of your ship.

CATCH THE WAVE – *Chapter Summary*

IMPORTANT POINTS TO REMEMBER

- Our world is experiencing tremendous change as we transition through a number of recurring universal cycles and events affecting humanity, the Earth, and our universe:
    - A 26,000-year cycle (a 12,000-year cycle of ascending consciousness—waking up/aware, and a 12,000-year period of descending consciousness—asleep/unaware)
    - Five eras of approximately 5,125 years, representing the Five Worlds or "Suns"
    - Twelve cycles of approximately 2,160 years representing the Great Zodiac Cycle
    - The occurrence of "The Great Alignment," which only happens once every 26,000 years. This is when the axis of our planet aligns perfectly with the center of our galaxy—the Milky Way.
- The world as we know it is ENDING. Yet, with every ending, there comes a NEW BEGINNING.
- The Earth will be the recipient of the effects caused by this transition well after December 21, 2012. We will witness:
    - Extreme weather and changes in weather patterns
    - Time speeding up
    - Increased natural disasters

How each of us fares during this transition (with ease or great difficulty), depends on how we prepare our mind, body, and soul.

- Astrology is the scientific study of the influence upon human affairs as well as terrestrial and celestial events, based on the position of the planets and stars.

- Our planet is shifting from the Age of Pisces to the Age of Aquarius
- The Age of Aquarius is known as the Age of Enlightenment. It is considered a time for the awakening of the human consciousness and for the influx and/or unfolding of information in all fields of reality.

ACTION STEPS
- Continue your education. There is a ton of information surrounding the shift in cycles. Exercise due diligence. As you continue your research, rely on your heart and your truth will reveal itself. Investigate the awesome science that is astrology. It is truly a profound study.
- Release the FEAR around the "End of the World" prophesies. No one can perform his or her best coming from a position of fear.
- Have your astrological chart prepared by a professional astrologer. You will be amazed at the information revealed.

LIFE LESSONS FOR TRANSFORMATION

Learning that the Earth and humanity are experiencing a natural transition was truly life-changing for me. I was able to release an immense load of fear surrounding the "End of the World" prophecies. How did this release of fear show up in my life?

Currently, I find myself witness to the natural disasters, plaques, famine, and deaths that were prophesied. However, with new vision and understanding, I am no longer traumatized with fear and anxiety. While I watch with deep concern for the destruction and transition of lives, it is not with a mind questioning why (an angry) God allowed this to happen. Or being afraid of what's in store for me. It is amazingly liberating to free your mind of belief systems that don't serve you anymore, allowing you to raise your consciousness and react to your world from a place of peace, power, and control of your emotions.

The benefits of having your personal astrological chart prepared are numerous. The information ascertained will truly enhance your quest to "Know Thyself." Once you have your chart prepared, you will be able to Navigate Your Existence from a standpoint of "knowing." You will be privy to knowing the best time to look for that new job and if the stars are in the right position (or are the energies compatible) for you to get that job at this time. Or you may be looking to relocate and wondering which is the best city, state, or country. Or maybe you need to know about that new cutie—is he Mr. Right, or is she Miss Right? Is your astrological sign compatible?

This is just some of the information that may be gleaned from an astrological chart.

Uh-oh…Are those fears of "spookiness" sneaking in again? Remember that astrology is a science; there's nothing spooky about it. And from my experience, it is extremely accurate. But it is just a tool to assist us in the quest for self-knowledge. There are many ways to understand and connect to the core of our essence. Trust and go with your feelings.

RESTORE the Knowledge of the Ancestors

Chapter 4

Everything Is Connected

*P*RIOR TO GETTING UNDERWAY, ONE WOULD CERTAINLY WANT to know about the composition of the vessel: Are the parts made of wood, plastic, or metal? In addition, you would certainly want to understand the medium through which you are traveling. Is the water frozen or fluid?

No navigator would ever dream of planning a journey without understanding the intricacies of his vessel and the environment. So, too, must we understand the basic elements of our ship and the environment in which we exist—our world, our universe.

That takes us to the discussion of energy, physics, philosophy, and the realization that everything is connected. Having a grasp of this information will provide a more penetrating appreciation of the power you possess within and how to access it. First, we'll start with a mini-lesson and then move on to some deeper concepts in the next chapter.

Is this Statue Solid?

Okay, how many people do you know who took physics in school? Are you one of them? Let me ask another question: How many people do you know who were afraid to take physics? Were you one of the latter? I certainly was. With respect to the studies of higher science, biology was about as far as I was willing to go. In addition, the high school counselors steered African Americans away from the sciences. Low expectations to enroll in the sciences and low expectations to attend college became the standard. Made to feel or think that we would never be able to comprehend the higher sciences, apprehension became the norm.

Consequently, I always thought of physics and chemistry as out of my reach, out of my realm of capability. Overall, I possessed a working knowledge of the concepts, yet the truth be told, any discussion of physics would've generated some anxious reactions—that is, until the day I had my "aha" moment.

Living in Las Vegas in the 1970s, the only mall was very expensive, especially since it catered mostly to tourists. Having lived in New York City with more shopping choices and price ranges, I was never very excited or hopeful about my visits to the local mall in Vegas. I *still* couldn't find a great pair of shoes!

On this particular day, I stepped into the mall and it had been transformed. An exhibit titled "The Continuum" filled the entire length of the mall. Everything looked so interesting, with modern and futuristic exhibits. The mall looked as if it had been lifted out of Las Vegas and set down in a major progressive city. Brimming with excitement, it didn't feel like I was "in Kansas" anymore.

The exhibits consisted of various metaphysical phenomena featuring reincarnation, life after death, and karma, to name a few. As I perused the exhibits, a very large fluorescent sign caught my attention. At the top, in big letters, it read: "Is This Statue Solid?"

Now, again, at the time, I was a second-grade teacher, so the question intrigued me and piqued my interest. Walking toward the sign, the letters grew increasingly smaller, as if to draw people closer to the exhibit.

As I approached the exhibit, there was a large bust on display. It stood approximately two feet tall, made of thick wood, and it appeared to be very heavy. So, with deep reflection, I found myself pondering the question…"Is this statue solid?" My immediate response was, "How silly; what kind of question is that?"

We all remember the school science project with the ice. You know—ice is solid; water is liquid; and when it evaporates, it becomes gas. So, according to our science lessons in school, of course the statue is solid!

Meanwhile, I'm thinking to myself, "You certainly wouldn't want me to hit you with it!" However, upon reading the rest of the sign, I received a lesson in physics that changed the perception of my very existence on this planet and in this universe. You may too, in just a minute, but let's pause for a moment to consider the constitution of atoms.

Teeny, Teeny, Tiny

What is physics, anyway? Simply put, it is the study of matter and energy. Matter is what things are made of and anything that takes up space. Now, if you break an object down to its smallest component, you will have an atom.

We all remember that an atom has the nucleus in the center consisting of the positively charged protons and the neutral neutrons, with the negatively charged electrons circulating around the nucleus with vigorous activity. The particles, neutrons, protons, and electrons constitute the matter, and the energy supplies the vigorous activity.

AN ATOM
All Matter Consists of Atoms

An atom is like a tiny solar system. In the center of the atom is the nucleus which is a cluster of protons and neutrons. The protons possess a positive charge, while the neutrons are electrically neutral. The negatively charged electrons circulate around the nucleus at tremendous speeds.

Navigate Your Existence!

If you take any item, such as a piece of wood, and you break it down to its smallest component that constitutes it being wood (as opposed to its *smallest* component, an atom, which would not distinguish it from any other object), you would have the molecule for wood. The wood is "wood" because of a specific combination of atoms that have attached to each other by the negative electrons and the positive proton particles.

OK, still with me? Good! Now back to the mall in Vegas so you can share my "aha" moment and understand why it's important for you to know this on your journey.

Well, the realization I experienced next just blew my mind. The exhibit displayed a diagram of an atom depicting the proportion of the particles (neutrons, protons, and electrons) and the space therein relevant to the size of the atom.

In order to appreciate what the display depicted, I want you to picture a football stadium. It's really a pretty massive structure. Next, imagine that you have a green pea. Hold it in between your forefinger and your thumb and walk out to the fifty-yard line. Place the green pea right in the middle of the football field. Then walk back to the stands.

Go all the way to the top of the stands and look around the circumference of the football stadium. Imagine that the green pea is the nucleus of the atom. The electrons would be circulating at the circumference of the football stadium. That is how much space is in each atom.

Every atom consists of a relatively small amount of matter (particles) in comparison to how much space it occupies. In addition, these particles are moving, circulating, and vibrating at tremendous speeds. Take a moment and let that sink in.

Once I attained a true appreciation of an atom's composition, I looked at the statue again. I stared at it intently, trying to see the space and movement within each atom. I couldn't see any space between the particles, nor could I see the movement, but now I was aware of both. This presented a serious challenge to my current understanding of "solid."

AN ATOM COMPARED TO A FOOTBALL FIELD

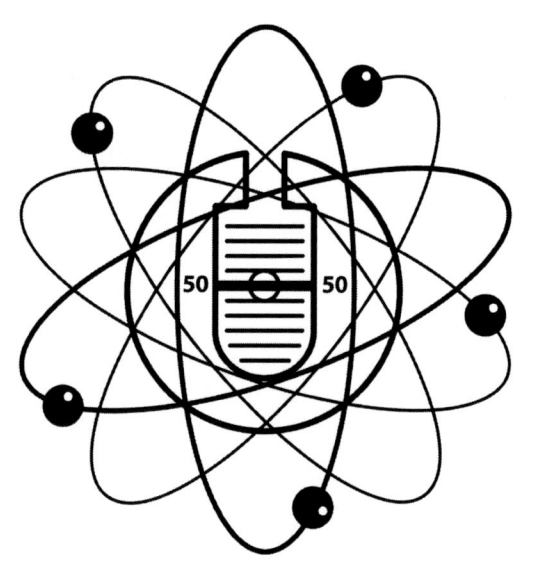

Each Atom consists of a relatively small amount of matter (particles) in comparison to how much space it occupies. Thus, SOLID is but an ILLUSION of our Earthy Perception.

Webster's defines *solid* as…"relatively firm or compact—not a liquid or a gas." Certainly, the statue was not liquid or gas. I always thought that *solid* meant that the particles of matter were so tightly compressed that there was no space in which anything could pass through. So much for my working understanding of physics.

And, oh my goodness…the science lesson I'd been teaching my students (ice is solid, water is liquid, etc.) was potentially incorrect or, at the very least, begged for further explanation. I was teaching my students the exact same lesson I had been taught in science, and the lesson I learned failed miserably to provide an accurate definition of *solid*.

Meanwhile, back at the exhibit, the illuminated sign proceeded to explain: "The solidness of the statue we 'see' is but an illusion of our earthly perception."

Boy, is that a mouthful. I understood the overall concept of illusion, because I now understood that the statue was not "solid," according my new level of awareness. Although scientists utilize the terms *solid, liquid*, and *gas* to describe the three states of matter, armed with new information, *solid* refers to a state in which matter or energy is vibrating so "slowly" that it appears to be solid.

That being said, I can hear some of you right now saying, "Well, which one is it? Are the particles in the atom vibrating at tremendous speeds, or so slowly that they appear solid?" The answer is both! It all depends on perception. We will revisit this issue in more depth a little later on in our journey.

But for now, let's continue on with our understanding of matter. Our third-dimensional world is defined in the geometrical concepts of length, width, and height, allowing humans to experience the statue through our senses. We can see it with our vision, but our earthy vision is not capable of seeing the space. We can touch it, but our sense of touch cannot feel the movement.

These explanations really helped me understand the statement about solidness being an illusion. However, it took me years to comprehend the statement at a more profound level. All in all, this one "aha" moment set me on a path to envision my world from a whole new perspective. After this experience, I would forever view my world through a different set of lenses.

Everything Is Made of the Same Stuff

There's your mini physics lesson. For me, it transformed my thinking about our third-dimensional planet. Everything is made of the same stuff: matter (particles) and energy (capacity for vigorous activity). By understanding the concept of an atom, therein lies the understanding to physics (matter) and (energy).

Okay, so let's look at this from another perspective. In our three-dimensional physical world, an atom is the basic component from which everything is comprised. This concept is based on physics, which is the study of matter and energy. An atom is comprised of matter and energy. Then, based on physics, everything in our physical world is made of the same stuff.

Go ahead…take a moment and look at everything around you. From the chair you are sitting in and the car you're driving to the trees you just passed and the person crossing the street, it's all comprised of the same stuff! The more profound our comprehension of these concepts, the more intense our transformation in how we relate to the world.

I know this is physics at its simplest level, but it gives us a working understanding of how our third-dimensional planet functions. Actually, I could get more detailed—in fact, science is certainly discovering more about our world every day, rendering our current knowledge null and void, or at least questionable.

For example, quantum physicists have examined an atom and its particles (electrons, protons, and neutrons), determining that each particle also consists of smaller particles. In turn, the definition of an atom being the smallest component of matter becomes a false statement.

But we're not going delve into that issue. However, it's food for thought to make you wonder about the universe in which we exist. Everything's made of the same stuff—matter and energy.

So, then, what distinguishes us from …a rock? It has to do with the level of awareness and/or consciousness, and that's an entirely different issue. A little further on in our journey, we will examine the concept of energy and stages of consciousness on a more profound level. For now, we will continue our exploration of everything being made of the same stuff.

Eastside/Westside

This takes me back to when I was in college. During my days at the State University of New York at Stony Brook, I had been introduced to this concept of everything being connected and made of the same stuff, but from a different perspective. I was getting my courses lined up for the semester when a very good friend named Oba said, "You have got to take this course." It was a 500, upper-level philosophy course.

Oba was a senior and a philosophy major while I was sophomore and an aspiring education major. Taking an upper-level philosophy course didn't seem like a great idea to me. Then he said, "This class is an easy 'A'." Well, now he had my full attention. Oba explained that the professor did not require a term paper or a mid-term exam. A final exam was the only requirement, and Oba promised he would work with me. Well, I was in.

The memory of the first day of class is indelibly etched in my mind. I arrived only to find, to my dismay, a new professor had been assigned to the course. So much for an easy "A."

The professor opened his briefcase, handed out an extensive course syllabus, and began his lecture. I panicked. From his thick East Indian accent, to the high-level philosophy concepts, I couldn't understand a word he was saying. I was ready to run for the hills, but there was something he said that made me stay. He stated something to the effect that "everything is connected" and "God is in everything." This caught my attention and really piqued my curiosity.

Although I had left the Baptist church some years earlier, the Western concept of religion remained embedded in my consciousness, with the perception of God as an external entity and each of us humans existing as separate and individual. Hence, the statements "everything is connected," and "God is in everything" gave me cause to wonder, especially since I had no frame of reference for this manner of thinking.

The philosophy course provided an introduction to Eastern philosophy and a comparison between both Eastern and Western philosophical perspectives, resulting in the expansion of my horizons. I likened the experience to living on one side of a doorway all my life, accepting existence as is, or as it was presented, and then one day opening the door and being exposed to the other side, to a completely different view of the world and a whole new perspective. It was like walking through a portal, opening new gateways of understanding for the navigation of my existence.

Let's pause here for a moment for an overview of what I learned in that life-altering class and see how it offers you an invaluable leg of your journey.

Philosophy is the study of the most fundamental questions that humankind has asked for centuries regarding reality and the principles underlying conduct, thought, and the nature of the universe. Our philosophical perceptions give rise to our thoughts on God and our religious beliefs.

The following chart offers a general comparison between the religious beliefs of Eastern and Western philosophy. I share this as an overall guideline since it is not inclusive of all religions or all perspectives of Eastern and Western philosophy. This information really helped me to initiate the transition to focusing within, consequently allowing me to harness powers that existed within me all along. As we continue on our path, you will see why it's important to comprehend this shift in order to Navigate Your Existence.

If this is your first introduction to the comparison between Western and Eastern philosophy, don't try to digest it all at once. There is a lot of information and it can be overwhelming. Just bring an open mind and be willing to expand your comfort zone; it never hurts to be exposed to a different point of view. After all, our beliefs create our reality, and everyone has the right to his or her own beliefs.

Comparing Eastern and Western Religions	
Eastern Religions: Hinduism (Advaita Vedanta) and Buddhism	Western ("Abrahamic") Religions: Judaism, Christianity, Islam

On What There Is	
Eastern Religions	Western Religions
Monism (one kind of reality)	Dualism (two kinds of reality, material and non-material)
All sentient beings have value (since they might be reincarnated souls), but their "otherness" is nevertheless illusory.	Sharp distinctions are made between humans and the rest of the natural world (things, animals) and between humans and other spirits (angels).

On Divine Nature (the nature of God)	
Eastern Religions	Western Religions
The Divine is imminent in creation (not separate). There are no words for the Divine.	The Divine is transcendent, essentially different from creation. "Father" imagery common.

On Creation and Change	
Eastern Religions	Western Religions
"Beginning" and "end" of the universe pose "questions that do not edify."	Eschatological outlook (God created the universe and will end it someday).
Change is considered an integral part of creation and does not indicate inferior or degraded being.	As in Plato, change is associated with degradation and disintegration, especially of the body. Perfect things (e.g., God) are changeless ("immutable").
Karma – the universal law of cause and effect – imposes forensic continuity: i.e., people get what they deserve as part of the very nature of reality. Every birth is the result of previous karma.	The human world is emphatically not the arena in which we play out our moral destiny: we get rewarded or punished for our earthly misdeeds only after we are dead, in another realm of being.

On Human Nature

Eastern Religions	Western Religions
The individual is not really real; the separateness of humans from creation and from one another is an illusion to be overcome.	The individual remains the same individual through eternity. The ontological separateness of the individual from others and from creation is real and permanent.
Human nature is essentially ignorant. We become better by becoming more enlightened.	Human nature is essentially sinful. We become better by willing control of our sinful impulses.
The human body is an illusion and is morally a distraction, but is not inherently bad.	The human body is seen as a major source of temptation, sin, change, decay. There is intense ambivalence toward the body.
Eastern religions feature well-developed traditions of bodily practices to attain enlightenment (e.g., yoga, breathing techniques, tai chi, tantra). Asceticism (punishment and bodily deprivation) is unusual in Eastern religions.	Because of the dualist separation of soul from body and systematic suspicion of body, few spiritual practices involve the body, aside from e.g., fasting and dietary rules. Instead, the believer is often urged to chastise and discipline the body through ascetic practice.
The good life consists of following *dharma* (personal duty, which is believed to be one with universal order and harmony).	The good life consists of obeying the laws of God and reason (the "natural law").

| Hinduism is radically non-egalitarian: you are born into a certain caste and must adhere to the rules of your sex and caste. Buddhism is egalitarian for men, but women are considered inferior. | The Western tradition is moderately egalitarian for men. Women and children generally have lower status. |

| *On Enlightenment* ||
Eastern Religions	Western Religions
The source of enlightenment and liberation is *within* the individual.	In Western religions, prophets, popes, mullahs, etc., convey God's word to ordinary people. Some forms of Protestantism, however, (e.g., Quakerism) emphasize looking within.
Many paths to enlightenment exist. Much spiritual practice is aimed at quieting the mind to allow enlightenment to happen.	Spiritual practice is often aimed at developing and maintaining personal relationship with God.

On Life and Death	
Eastern Religions	Western Religions
Reincarnation (transmigration of souls through many lifetimes) is a central belief. Because you know you'll be coming back, and the law of karma will automatically reward the good and punish the evil in the next incarnation, there is not a lot of philosophical worry about injustice and victimization (it's always temporary and never fatal).	"You only go around once." The problem of evil is thus huge in Western philosophy of religion. Also, sin is a much more serious matter, since you get only one chance at life. Heaven is for humans only, so the Western view is "species-ist." Animals don't get saved, nor do their interests matter much, whereas for non-Western religions, every sentient being eventually gets released.
The goal of the afterlife is release from ignorance, and ultimately, loss of self and merger with the Divine.	The goal of the afterlife is release from the body; the self remains the same self through eternity.
After-life traditions vary: *moksha* (liberation from the cycle of reincarnation); *nirvana* (blowing out the flame of desire), or the compassionate bodhisattva ideal.	Virtuous Mohammed, Jesus, and saints as role models.

Author: Sandy LaFave – Instructor, West Valley College, Saratoga, CA

This was my first introduction to Eastern religion and to the comparison between Western and Eastern spirituality. The two philosophies tend to contrast concepts, overlap others, and sometimes the concepts are similar but viewed from a different outlook.

During the course of the class, I acquired an overall understanding of most of the concepts. Some I didn't understand, and still others I was not ready to accept. It was much later, after years of research, before I was really able to grasp the profound esoteric connotations.

Yet the most profound lesson I acquired from the class was the notion of Oneness—a concept that there is only the One or the All—and in that Oneness, in the All, is an awareness and a consciousness that brings order to everything.

Now, the concept that everything is made of the same stuff and that "God" is in EVERYTHING started to make more sense. Now I could begin to conceive the notion that the Life Force, Source Energy, God Source, or God, was in everything, INCLUDING ME! Wow!

This new level of awareness allowed me to comprehend the second concept that I found remarkable: that the power we seek lies within. Traditionally, from a Western perspective, we were taught to search externally for our salvation. In this class, I learned to search within. What a concept—talk about an "aha" moment!

Everything happens for a reason. It was no accident that Oba steered me toward that class. I stayed in the class, struggled with the concepts, didn't get it all, but the introduction to Eastern philosophy changed my life. And, yes, I passed the class with a "C"…on my own.

It provided me with an introduction to the Oneness of our universe. Yet, it was another three-to-four years before I would experience "The Continuum" …"Is This Statue Solid?" mall exhibit, which provided a deeper understanding of physics, the study of matter and energy, and how it all relates to our world and our universe.

My new-found appreciation of physics from "The Continuum" exhibit escalated my understanding of how everything is connected. It took my awareness of Eastern and Western philosophy to a much more profound level. I now possessed a more in-depth awareness of my world and the universe.

The concept that everything is made of the same stuff became that much more apparent. So did the idea that "God" or that life force, that awareness, or that intelligence that holds it all together is in everything, even the rock. I began to look less and less for answers from external forces. Still, I wasn't exactly sure how to access the answers from within. Nor had I acquired a grasp of the concept of awareness, of consciousness on different levels. This "aha" was yet to come. But I was on the path…and the journey continues.

Stretching one's comfort zone or trekking in unfamiliar territory can become somewhat stressful. I guess I always found myself out on the edge of the norm, because I was always asking questions. However, that is how you learn.

By stretching the limits, you broaden your horizons. It puts you one step closer to getting out of the box—that box of limitation—the box filled with all the belief systems and "-isms" of our traditional educational, religious, political, and/or societal institutions.

To that end, it is not easy being introduced to notions that are, in many cases, opposite views from which you were raised—especially so many at one time. I have been on this journey for a long time. Fortunately, I was introduced to various concepts in bits and pieces, affording me some time to let things sink in. As I share with you some of my experiences, it is my hope that it will help you to more readily visualize, conceptualize, and internalize the material covered within these pages.

The more profound my understanding about energy, the more intense was the transformation. As I evolved in my perception of energy—as thought, as mind, as source, as creation, as God—so too was my evolution in how I perceived my world. Not only did my world views change, but the way I interact with life changed.

God is in Everything

It was a Sunday morning, and I was attempting to explain the Eastern philosophical concept that God exists in everything to my two sons. Although I had discussed this concept with them previously, they maintained a belief in the Western concept of God as an anthropomorphic being, existing externally somewhere "up in heaven." For the most part in America, Western philosophy is prevalent in the schools and institutions and it is difficult not to be exposed to the concepts.

My oldest son questions everything. I wonder where he acquired that trait? At any rate, I had just finished giving it my best shot at explaining the notion that God is in everything, when my son chimed in, "So, Mommy, that means God is in the trash can?"

I think all the blood drained out of my face since I had to figure out how to respond to that question. I took a deep breath, looked at my son, and replied, "Yes, son, God is even in the trash can."

As he sat there with a smirk on his face, delighted with himself that he got me to say this seemingly ridiculous statement, I quickly responded, "Because God don't make no junk!" That did make me feel better as I continued to try and explain energy and why God was in the trash can.

"God is in everything" is an abstract concept and difficult to grasp, especially if you've not yet been introduced to Eastern philosophy. All in all, shifting our mindset is a process. It takes time, continued research, and experience with each new idea.

Understanding physics at its core was such a tremendous value to me. It allowed me to broaden my horizons enough to incorporate the concept of Oneness into my life. Now I can understand notions like (there is only one) and (we are not separate individuals but all connected). No, I didn't take physics in school, but I know people who did. And, still, they have no understanding of the concepts I share with you today. Understanding physics and energy opened up the possibility for me to change my perspective on death and dying.

Energy Never Dies; It Just Changes

As you may recall, my first experience with the concept of *"Life After Life"* occurred with the death of my grandmother. She had died early that morning. Later that evening she appeared in my bedroom in the upper right-hand corner. I couldn't see her; I couldn't hear her; but I could feel her presence and knew she was there. And she let me know she was just fine.

So, here again, having been raised in the Western tradition, I was taught that when you die, you are dead. Well, this experience with my grandmother proved to me, contrary to all of my previous teachings, that life existed after "death." This inspired a complete conversion in my thinking on death and dying. Over the years, as I learned more about energy and our universe, my views continued to evolve. I embraced concepts like "Energy never dies, it just changes," and "There is no such thing as death."

"Of course you don't die. Nobody dies. Death doesn't exist. You only reach a new level of vision, a new realm of consciousness, a new unknown world. – Henry Miller

Knowledge is power. This information has forever changed how I process death and dying. And this is from one who has had a lot of practice, since so many of my family and friends have transitioned. See, I even changed how I speak about death, now referring to it as what it is—a *transition* of energy.

My "grieving" process is shorter and easier now that I understand that life is but a continuum. Certainly, it's still difficult; we just don't want to let go, knowing we will miss our loved ones. Yet the word *freedom* comes to mind when being able to release the hurt, pain, and stress more quickly and begin the healing process. Grieving is such a personal issue, and we all have our ways in which to cope. It is my deepest wish that this information helps you even the slightest bit on your journey.

CATCH THE WAVE – *Chapter Summary*

IMPORTANT POINTS TO REMEMBER

- Everything is made of the same stuff—energy. And it's all connected.
- Energy is everything, and everything is energy.
- NO! That statue is NOT solid.
- SOLID is but an illusion of our earthly perception.
- There is only ONE source—Oneness, from which all else emanates.
- Oneness, or Source Energy, or that which we call God, is in everyone and everything.
- Energy doesn't die; it just changes.
- Life is a continuum—there is no such thing as death.

ACTION STEPS

- Periodically gaze at a "solid" object. Try to "see" the atoms, the particles of matter, the movement, the space. This will help to remind you that our physical environment is an illusion. It will reinforce the notion that we are not separate from our neighbors or environment.

- Spend time reconnecting to nature. Talk a walk in the park; go to the mountains; or visit the lake/beach. Experience the energy and natural essence. Enjoy!
- Begin to look at your neighbors through different eyes, from a different perspective—one of connectedness versus separateness. So many of us don't even know our neighbors.
- If you've not done so, take an opportunity to explore Western and Eastern philosophies. I encourage you to keep an open mind.
- Revisit your thoughts on death and dying.

LIFE LESSONS FOR TRANSFORMATION

The concepts I encountered in this chapter presented life-altering experiences and the information was absolutely mind-boggling, especially having been reared in the culture of Western philosophy.

Is This Statue Solid?
Everything Is Made of the Same Stuff
God Is in Everything
Energy Never Dies; It Just Changes

To be able to conceptualize that our world is not "solid," but fluid and in constant motion.

To be able to comprehend the concept that the "solidness" we perceive is just an illusion of our earthly perception.

To realize that when you break an atom/matter down to its smallest, infinitesimal parts you have pure energy. And everything is made of energy. And therein lies God.

To come to the realization that energy never dies. You can't create it; you can't destroy it. You can only transmute it. Thus, there is no such thing as death.

These concepts completely eluded my capacity for understanding, until I experienced my "aha" moments. I don't know about you, but this is all so exciting to me! I feel a sense of freedom! Being released from the limiting beliefs that held my thoughts captive. Being freed of the long painful grieving process of "losing" loved ones. Now I know they are not lost and I know I can talk to them and keep them with me in spirit, if not in the flesh. I am so grateful to have been exposed to this knowledge, which prepared me for even more profound "aha" moments along my journey.

RESTORE the Knowledge of the Ancestors

Chapter 5

Now You See It – Now You Don't

So now what lies ahead? As we surge forward along our path, what are the forces, seen and unseen, that we might encounter and how might they affect our journey? Certainly we are aware of the tangible elements that could alter our course. But are there other unseen forces that impact us?

We can see waves with certainty and know they are real. But what about the forces that caused the wave? We can't see the wind, but we know of its effects on the water. What about the sun? We feel the heat of the day and can see the light, but can we detect the dangerous ultraviolet rays?

Then there's the infamous Bermuda Triangle. It is reported that dozens of ships and airplanes have disappeared while traveling through that area located in the Atlantic Ocean. Scientists are still baffled as to what causes the phenomenon. Many say it has to do with magnetic fields emanating from within the Earth's surface. Many a navigator traveling through the Bermuda Triangle has reported magnetic anomalies affecting their navigational instruments. Again, we cannot see magnetic fields, yet we are aware of their existence and effects.

Omniscient Forces

So too are there seen and unseen forces or realms in our world that influence our very being. As I began to comprehend physics on a more profound level, my new understanding allowed me to view my physical world from a deeper perspective.

I have always heard of the word *metaphysics* but really didn't understand what it meant. At first, I too equated it with the world of the occult or something spooky or "of the devil," since this is what I was taught through my religious upbringing. As we moved closer to the Age of Aquarius, the term *metaphysics* kept popping up, so I resorted to my Webster's Dictionary for an accurate definition.

Metaphysics is defined as the branch of philosophy that seeks to explain the nature of being and reality. This definition really didn't help. Eventually, another "aha" moment and another lesson in physics allowed me to comprehend the term *metaphysics*.

We'll get to that in a moment but let's begin by taking a closer look at the word *metaphysical:* meta-physical. The prefix *meta* means *after, beyond,* or *higher. Physical* is defined as "having material existence, perceptible through the senses and subject to the laws of nature." So *metaphysical* really means *beyond the physical,* or "beyond that which we can experience with our five senses."

Let's make it simple. If you look at a ceiling fan in the off position, you can clearly see the five blades, correct?

SETTINGS ON A FAN

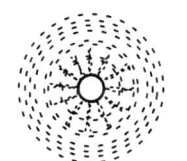

Fan – Super High Setting

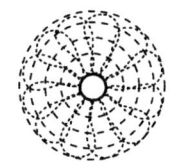

Fan – High Setting

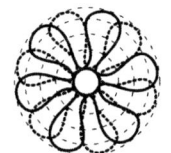

Fan – Medium Setting

Fan – Off Position

First, turn the fan to its lowest setting. The blades will begin to rotate, yet you can still see each individual blade. Next, turn the fan to the medium setting and watch as the blades begin to blend together. Finally, turn the fan to the highest setting. The individual blades seem to have disappeared.

Let's say there was a super-high setting. Would you be able to "see" the blades at all at this setting? Probably not. Would you be able to "feel" the effects of the blades? Very much so.

Let's examine the word *metaphysical* a little closer. *Physical* is the part of our world that we are aware of, that we perceive to be real. It is the part that we can experience through our five senses; that we can see, feel, smell, hear, or taste.

As noted earlier, the prefix *meta* means *after, beyond,* or *higher.* Subsequently, *metaphysical* is the world *beyond* the physical (matter) that we cannot "see" or perceive with our five senses. Yet, we are still subject to the effects of the metaphysical world. Aha! It's all so simple.

For those who are just not sold on the fact that there are unseen forces that affect us and our world, let's take a quick trip through the realm of gravity. If it goes up, it must come down. This is the simple law of gravity.

By the way, we all remember that time in our childhood when we tried to defy the laws of gravity, trying to jump up and stay up. We searched and searched to find some way to defy the laws of gravity and "stay up" but couldn't find one possibility. Even an airplane has to come down eventually.

Finally, we had to accept the law as real. With gravity, you can't see it, touch it, taste it, hear it, or feel it, but you know it exists. And there is no question that gravity has an effect on your life, your very existence.

In order to comprehend the next discussion, we will need to broaden our perspective on energy. It's time—prepare to stretch that comfort zone! Grab hold of the rafters, as the ship increases in velocity.

Everything is Energy

It is imperative you understand that EVERYTHING in the UNIVERSE is ENERGY. That includes every…*thing, thought, emotion, action, experience,* and so forth.

Let's take a closer look. An atom is the basic unit of existence for our third-dimensional world. Of course it is comprised of matter and energy. The components of the atom, (the electrons, neutrons, and protons), constitute the matter and the vigorous force is the energy, or *conscious force.*

Conscious force?

That brings us to a new discussion: Energy is aware; energy is conscious; energy is thought. And out of thought comes everything or energy.

I know; it's a lot if you are new to these concepts. Okay, think of this: "In the beginning was the Word." Or look at the term that describes EVERYTHING: *universe* or *uni-verse*, meaning *one word.*

Energy (or thought) gives rise to matter, or *solidified thought.* Think of this as the vibration of energy (or thought) slowing down enough to condense into a particle. Energy itself is comprised of particles, or solidified thought. At a subatomic level, these particles are so minuscule that humans can't see or even begin to comprehend them.

At our third-dimensional level, we "see" energy in the form of atoms. The atoms have particles or (solidified thought) "large" enough and circulating "slow" enough so that our five senses can experience their existence.

This takes us back to the question of whether the atoms in the statue were moving quickly or slowly. Remember that my response was "both," depending on the perspective? Viewing the statue utilizing our five senses, the particles in the atom are moving quite slowly—so slowly that they have condensed into what we perceive to be solid. In the same respect, understanding the physics of atoms, we must appreciate the speed in which the particles (the neutrons, protons, and electrons) are traveling. So again, depending on our perspective, it can be said that the particles within each atom are traveling at great speeds or quite slowly.

All energy is conscious. Conscious simply means *aware*. Every form of energy "knows" exactly what it is doing. Thus, the phrase: God (or conscious energy) is in everything.

We will cover conscious thought again and in more detail in the next chapter. For some, this may be a tough concept to grasp. By the same token, it took me a little bit to comprehend this notion.

Fortunately, I was exposed to these concepts through various "aha" moments over a period of years—hence, affording me time to process new perceptions before being exposed to the next wave of knowledge. Similarly, if you are not familiar with many of these concepts, it can be a little overwhelming. However, given the times we find ourselves in, there is no time to waste. So batten down the hatches and hold on. As we continue to open new portals of understanding, the concepts begin to overlap and become more apparent. Hang in there.

Seven Dimensions

Let's go back to the song "Age of Aquarius," which was really titled "Aquarius/Let the Sun Shine In." Do you remember the name of the group? Yes, The Fifth Dimension. Again, just as most people had no idea what the song really meant, I'm sure even fewer had an inkling of the concept of a *fifth dimension*.

As a matter of fact, I had no clue what fifth dimension meant in the '60s and wouldn't figure it out for decades to come. At the time, my only understanding of dimensions was what I learned in geometry class. More specifically, we were introduced to our world of matter in the three dimensions of length, width, and height.

Continuing my study of metaphysics, I came across the notion of *seven* dimensions. Hmm…First, I was introduced to the perception of our three-dimensional world, then exposed to the term *fifth dimension*, though I still had no idea what it meant, and now I'm hearing that there are seven dimensions. This new information was intriguing, though at this point, still meaningless to me. Nonetheless, I was eager to become enlightened on the subject.

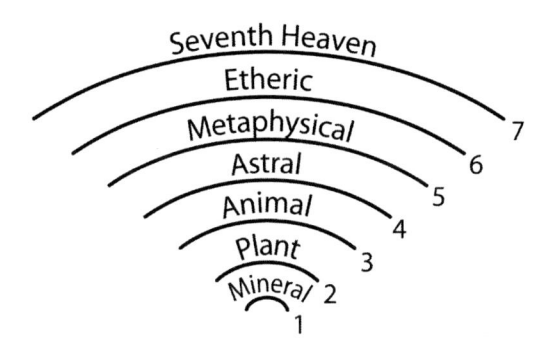

```
     Seventh Heaven
        Etheric
      Metaphysical      7
        Astral        6
        Animal       5
        Plant       4
       Mineral    3
                  2
                 1
```

SEVEN DIMENSIONS

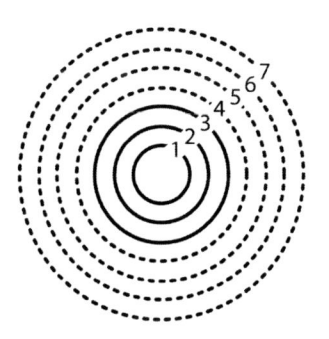

Each dimension carries its own frequency.
Energy is conscious respectively at each level.
The Physical World consists of the first three
dimensions. The fourth dimension is a gateway
to the higher dimensions. *The Metaphysical
World* consists of dimensions five through seven.

Now is the time to pull the content regarding the "fan" segment to the forefront of your mind. This section is going to require that you really trust in the possibility of an unseen realm. Consequently, you will be called on to deal with that which may be unfamiliar to you and that which you cannot see.

As with all of our topics, the information we are about to delve into is ancient; thus, it has been subject to various interpretations and variations over the eons. Please allow me to share some of the information I've uncovered along my journey and my perception of the dimensions.

First, we begin by distinguishing the concept of dimensions that we learned in geometry class from the discussion of seven dimensions. The common understanding of dimensions refers to space (as in taking up space). It is defined in terms of length, width, and height and used to describe our three-dimensional world.

With respect to the discussion of the seven dimensions, the term *dimension* describes the frequency or speed at which matter, energy, or thought vibrates and is conscious. Or, in other words, *dimension* refers largely to the vibration of the energy or solidified thought (matter) within that realm.

As we forge onward, there are seven levels or dimensions that encompass our earthly/heavenly realm. We now understand that everything in our world and universe is made of the same "stuff" or energy, which includes every thought, word, object, experience, or emotion. In addition, all energy has its own vibration, and its frequency can be measured. As energy becomes more aware or conscious, it increases in vibration and is able to ascend through the dimensions.

What? Well, to understand this better, let's start with the first three dimensions that are familiar to us.

Our planet Earth is comprised of three dimensions. The first level is the mineral kingdom, the second level is the plant kingdom, and third level is the animal/human kingdom. All three levels are the *phys-*

ical levels. Again, at the physical levels, energy in the form of atoms is "moving" or vibrating so slowly that it gives the illusion of a solid mass. Thus, we get to experience energy through our five senses. We can think of these three dimensions as being on the lower settings of the "fan," wherein we can see the blades.

First Dimension – Mineral Kingdom

The First Dimension is the mineral or rock kingdom. The low vibration results in a solidifying of thought (energy) into the form of matter. At this level, life force energy or consciousness exists in the atom. It expresses itself through the laws of gravity, magnetism, and chemical elements.

Second Dimension – Plant Kingdom

In the plant kingdom, life forms into a carbon-based existence utilizing sunlight and the mineral kingdom to sustain itself. The vibrational frequency is at a higher realm. At this level, consciousness is capable of reproduction.

Third Dimension – Animal/Human Kingdom

The vibrational frequency continues to increase in the animal kingdom. Consciousness becomes more complex, ranging from the simple life forms to the more advanced human stage. Life at this level is also carbon-based and capable of reproduction. It is the innate intelligence of humans that distinguishes us from the rest of creation.

It is the first, second, and third dimensions that constitute our physical world. The three aspects of length, width, and depth are what define the construct or matrix of our reality. In other words, it is the slowness of the particles in the atoms and the density of this realm that cause us to perceive items as real, or solid. As humans, we experience this third-dimensional world by utilizing our five senses. This is why our "energy" needs a physical body to navigate this world.

We have—located within the physical body—a light body of energy that awaits ascension. As all energy is conscious, the energy that is you has a natural desire to ascend (or return) to the higher realms. In addition, each dimension is likened to a school where there are lessons to be learned and experiences to encounter. As we learn the necessary lessons, we are able to ascend. The more we concentrate on our external bodies and entertaining our five senses, the lower our vibration.

Focusing *within* on our light bodies leads to a higher vibration, raising our awareness/consciousness and increasing the potential to rise to higher dimensions. At higher dimensions, the vibrational frequency increases, and matter gives way to pure energy—energy with particles so miniscule that we cannot even comprehend their existence, similar to the fan on higher settings. The higher the dimension, the faster the setting on the fan. The Fourth Dimension is considered a gateway to the higher or more celestial realms.

Fourth Dimension – Astral Plane

Astral means elevated in station. This dimension is known as the gateway between the physical (seen) and the metaphysical (unseen) dimensions. It is home to those disembodied souls who are not ready to transition to the higher celestial dimensions. Again, each dimension is like a grade level in school with lessons to learn. Those who are not ready cannot move on to higher grades. A fourth variable, *time*, is added to length, width, and height in the Fourth Dimension.

Einstein defines time itself as the Fourth Dimension in his Theory of Relativity. This fourth variable allows for souls to travel back and forth through *time* and experience the past and the future. This affords us an opportunity to remember who and what we are, and where we've come from. We'll talk a little more on that later.

Although this is a higher realm than the Third Dimension, souls at this level have issues with duality, seeing things as good/evil, hot/cold, and male/female, which are views brought with them from the Third Dimension. Both third-and fourth-dimensional beings must transition from thinking in terms of duality to the realization that there is no separation…there is only oneness. One must master true unconditional love at this level, which includes forgiveness. Unconditional love and forgiveness are the keys for entrance into the Fifth Dimension.

Fifth Dimension – Metaphysical Realm

The Fifth Dimension is the realm of the metaphysical—beyond the physical. Time exists only within each individual's consciousness. This realm requires a higher frequency, or a higher evolution. You must raise your fourth-dimensional spiritual/astral vibration to the higher-faster level in order to enter the Fifth Dimension.

The Fifth Dimension is a higher frequency of spiritual evolvement, which requires one to be purified, released from all fear and negativity, and maintain control over mental and emotional issues. Entrance into the Fifth Dimension requires that you learn to manage your energy, your mind, and your heart.

You must learn to control your thoughts. You must be responsible for the quality of your thoughts, keeping them in a positive, high vibration, because you create what you think. In other words, your thoughts become things. And, in the Fifth Dimension and higher levels, your thoughts manifest into *things* with tremendous speed.

In the Fifth Dimension and above, your soul must reside in a vibration of love—unconditional love for all and everything.

Sixth Dimension – Etheric Dimension

The existence at this level is considered etheric or gaseous where the energy is vibrating at such a high intensity it is light as air. New colors and sounds are integrated into existence at this realm, and new forms of creation are possible. Much of existence at this level is out of the range of comprehension for humans. We have enough on our hands achieving residence in the Fifth Dimension. The Sixth Dimension is a bridge to the higher celestial realm of the Seventh Dimension.

Seventh Dimension – Seventh Heaven

The concept of the Seventh Dimension is not that unfamiliar to many of us. We have all heard of this place, though we may not have completely understood. We know it as *Seventh Heaven*. It's been said to be a place so wonderful that it is compared to the epitome of having a great experience ("I was so happy, I was in Seventh Heaven.") It's the place most of us pray that our souls will find as the "final" resting place.

The Seventh Dimension is the highest form of spiritual growth that can be comprehended by most earthly beings. It forms the outermost concentric ring around the Earth and is considered to be the home base to the most of the angels and Ascended Masters, such as Jesus, Buddha, El, Ra, the Orisha, and others. The Seventh Dimension vibrates at a frequency of pure love and universal wisdom. We've also heard: "In my father's house there are many *mansions*." Are the mansions referring to the dimensions?

So now do you see why I suggested you recall the information about the "fan" to the forefront? This section requires belief in that which may be unknown, unseen, and/or outside of your present perception. However, I always believed there was a heaven. I always believed there was a God. Yet, I could not see either. If this segment requires you to stretch your imagination, then go for it. There's more to come. Remember, the more you expand your realm of consciousness, the more information flows in your direction.

Transition to a Fifth-Dimensional Planet

Now, with an overall understanding of the Seven Dimensions, we can approach this next issue. Earth is transitioning from a third-dimensional planet to a fifth-dimensional planet. That makes one ask, "What? How? Why?"

In the first chapter we discussed in great detail many of the changes our planet is experiencing—changes we have already experienced, changes that are unfolding every day, and changes foretold of events to come.

Just as a quick review:

Earth is experiencing the ENDING and BEGINNING of various Cycles:

The Great Zodiac Cycle – 26,000-year cycle

The Five Worlds (or Suns) – Five 5,125-year cycles

The Zodiac Cycle –The Transition from the
   Age of Pisces to the Age of Aquarius

The Great Galactic Alignment

All of these events have to do with the movement of the celestial bodies that affect our Earth, causing major changes. As these bodies move into various positions, they affect the energy that encompasses our earthly/heavenly realm. These changes not only affect the Earth but the regions above that include the dimensions.

As the energy shifts, the vibrations are increasing, thus changing the frequency of dimensions. As the vibrations of our third-dimensional planet increase, they are causing the Third Dimension to collapse (or merge) with the Fourth Dimension. This is happening NOW.

We are actually experiencing this phenomenon as evidenced in our references regarding time, such as "Boy, where did the time go?" or "Time sure is flying by." Time really, truly is speeding up as the Earth's vibration accelerates. Earth's energy is changing. Very soon the Earth will no longer be a third-dimensional planet. The frequencies of the Third Dimension and the Fourth Dimension are collapsing together, and the Earth will soon be vibrating at the fifth-dimensional frequency.

What does this mean for humanity? In order to exist in fifth-dimensional frequency, we will have to increase our vibrations and our level of consciousness. That may be a short sentence and sound simple, but the process is profound.

As the earth transitions through this period of change, so too will humanity have to change. The frequency and vibration of the Fifth Dimension will require that we change our habits.

No longer can we ingest heavy non-nutritious foods and expect our vibration to increase. Fried chicken, mac 'n cheese, candied yams, collard greens, and cornbread. Ummm, sounds delicious, but it is the very menu that will keep us grounded in the Third Dimension.

Fifth-dimensional frequency requires you:
- To eat light; eat live foods, fresh fruits and vegetables
- To increase your water intake
- To move your body and get exercise
- To practice deep breathing and/or meditation

A major requirement for becoming commensurate with fifth dimensional energy is to control your thoughts and emotions. This means releasing all fear, judgment, and negative thoughts. The Fifth Dimension exists in a realm of unconditional love. The vibration and frequency is so high that your thoughts are manifested in an instant. Thus the saying, "Thoughts are things."

That is to say, whatever you are thinking you will manifest and attract that element to you. If you are harboring fears or negative thoughts, that is what will manifest and engulf you. I can't imagine anyone who would want to dwell in such an existence. In addition, I don't think I know of anyone who has mastered controlling all thought and emotion. This is why there is no time to waste. We all must begin to prepare now.

The Fifth Dimension brings forth the "best of the best" or the "worst of the worst." The beauty of it all is that no one is responsible for how you fare through this monumental time. You are the conductor of your ship. The onus is upon *you* to manifest the existence you desire. Residence in the Fifth Dimension requires ascension of your consciousness to a higher vibration of unconditional love. It is up to you to Navigate Your Existence through the Third Dimension and beyond.

The Times... They-Are-a-Changing

As we maneuver into this new space and time, observing Earth's metamorphosis can become a little unnerving and even a little scary. It's okay to have some apprehension. The truth is that I have my anxious moments, too. One only has to look around to see the changes the Earth is experiencing right before our very eyes.

A *tsunami*? Prior to December 26, 2004, many had never even heard the term. On that day, a tsunami (a massive wave) struck the coast of Indonesia and swept away 200,000 people. Wow! Now the term tsunami is quite prevalent in the minds and hearts of all who remember the incident.

Hurricane "Katrina," is a term indelibly cemented in everyone's memory, when the levies exploded and left much of New Orleans under water. In 2011, Japan experienced a 9.0 earthquake and the ensuing tsunami not only wreaked havoc, but also caused a meltdown

Omiyale Jubé

at the Fukushima nuclear plant. This disaster caught the attention of the world as radiation spread through the atmosphere and the oceans, causing damage of still unknown proportions.

The following year brought Hurricane Sandy to the Eastern seaboard of the United States in 2012. I watched in disbelief as I witnessed the tip of Manhattan in New York submerged in water. Unbelievable!

Snow in the spring; warm weather in the winter; scientists attempting to explain the concept of global warming; and the list continues. All of these occurrences have certainly made for interesting conversation with regard to the weather we've experienced lately on our changing Earth.

Currently, I live in Las Vegas, and the weather has changed drastically over the course of the last thirty years or so. It gives me reason to pause as I lie in my bed and listen to the winds howl through my backyard night after night. Years ago we would have some dust storms, but a consistent high wind in Vegas is certainly not the norm. Recently, we experienced a period of two months of unusually strong winds whipping through the valley.

What's even more disconcerting is, as I talked to friends and family across the country and mention these high winds, I repeatedly receive comments that it's been windy in their cities, too. Yes, the times…they-are-a-changing.

Consequently, it's only natural to have some anxious moments. But, again, one cannot perform optimally from a position of fear. The trick is not to stay there. It is difficult to witness the catastrophes and even more challenging for those who are affected by them. Acknowledge the occurrences, and then summon to mind that all of this is a part of Earth progressing to a higher dimension. Acknowledge the event, then let go of the fear.

It all comes back to preparation, to getting your ship in order. We do not have to drift at sea, with no course of direction. The universe has provided a system, or a framework, designed to guide us along the path through these times and these seemingly uncharted waters.

In the next chapter we will explore this framework, which lays out exactly the laws by which to direct your behaviors. It is time to chart your course, discover your internal compass, and Navigate Your Existence.

CATCH THE WAVE – *Chapter Summary*

IMPORTANT POINTS TO REMEMBER

- There are seen and unseen forces that affect our being and environment, whether we are aware of them or not.
- Metaphysical: *Meta* is a prefix meaning *beyond*; therefore, *metaphysical* simply means *beyond the physical,* or *beyond* that which we can perceive with our five senses. Metaphysical speaks to the unseen forces that impact our existence.
- Respect Nature. Consciousness exists at each of the seven dimensions.
- The goal of ascension through the dimensions is achieved through enlightenment. Enlightenment is achieved through raising your vibration and/or consciousness.
- Unconditional love is the key to the Fifth Dimension.
- Heaven exists on various levels and is a state of consciousness.

ACTION STEPS

- Prepare for the Fifth Dimension:
  - Eat light, live foods such as fresh fruits and vegetables
  - Increase your intake of water

- Exercise; move your body
- Breathe; practice meditation and/or deep breathing
* Open your heart to unconditional love
* Learn and practice the art of forgiveness:
  - Acknowledge the situation and the participants
  - What part did you play in creating/manifesting the situation? (Be as honest with yourself as possible.)
  - What lesson did you learn?
  - Forgive the persons involved
  - Forgive yourself
  - Let it go!

LIFE LESSONS FOR TRANSFORMATION

All things considered, at this time in our lives, the single most important charge is preparation for the Fifth Dimension. Evidence of our preparedness lies in the question, "Are you vibrating in the frequency of unconditional love?" As soon as one attains the vibration and frequency of unconditional love, all else will take care of itself.

With that in mind, it is important to note a major factor in achieving unconditional love is the art of forgiveness. To forgive is a process; the steps are noted in the Action Steps. Subsequently, it requires practice and time to incorporate this sense of being into your reality. Accordingly, it's easier said than done. Please allow me to share some of my personal encounters with "forgiveness."

In the midst of my travels, I came upon a most wonderful book entitled, *The Four Agreements* by Don Ruiz. It speaks of four accords and how knowledge of these agreements enables one to direct their course in life. Although all four are remarkable, the agreement "Don't Take It Personally" has had the greatest impact on my life—specifically, in my quest to attain unconditional love and learn forgiveness.

In brief, the concept surrounding "Don't take It personally" is as such: Many times when you feel a person has wronged you, it is because of an issue that individual is dealing with. It is not about you. So don't internalize the negativity or allow the incident to cause you to react negatively. It's not about you!

I had read *The Four Agreements* and was well aware of the concept "Don't take It personally." However, being cognizant of the concept and practicing it are two different things.

Case in point…I experienced a situation in which an associate had major issues with me for no apparent reason. In other words, she just didn't like me. For years she tried everything she could to cause me discomfort, yet never was able to ruffle my feathers.

Finally, the day came to pass when she achieved her mission. Her actions aggravated me so that I fussed and fussed for a two-week period. Then one day, right in the midst of a rant, I caught myself. All of a sudden the phrase "Don't take it personally" came into my head. I said to myself, "This is not about me."

Almost immediately and quite literally, I felt the angst melting away from my body. I took myself through the forgiveness process: I forgave my associate; I took responsibility for placing myself in the situation; and I forgave myself and assessed my lessons learned, one of them being the importance of forgiveness.

Well, you would think the lesson I learned that day would have stuck, but old habits die hard. It was maybe three-to-four years later when, once again, I found myself in an unpleasant situation. It involved a breach of contract and financial neglect, with me being the recipient.

Again, I was quite angry. I ranted and raved for forty-eight hours before I caught myself. Once again I remembered the phrase, took myself through the process of forgiveness, and let it go.

Now I would be remiss if I ended my tale here and neglected to share my latest incident. This incident centered on an individual who wanted to draw me into a confrontation. The conversation lasted about two minutes before I changed directions and refused to be pulled into a low-vibrational interchange. I did, however, hold onto the issue for about thirty minutes before I was totally through the process and let it go.

All of the aforementioned examples point out the power of forgiveness. It is critical to your well-being. How you process situations can be a determining factor in every aspect of your life. While holding on to unresolved issues, you are holding onto negative feelings, thoughts, and emotions, all the while creating stress and keeping you in a low vibrational frequency.

Of course this can affect your health and your emotional state, and creep into your other relationships, affecting your family and work environment. Most importantly, it is crucial that you forgive, so you can heal and raise your vibration. Ascension is achieved by raising your vibration. Remember, forgiveness is as much for you as it is for the others involved.

So, again, although I am well aware of the principles and possess the tools to raise my vibration, it is a process. With personal issues, you have to really dig deep into your resources and sometimes even call on like-minded persons to help keep the ship on course.

As previously noted, preparation for the fifth dimension is of the utmost importance. Residence requires a consciousness vibrating at the frequency of unconditional love and the pathway is through forgiveness. As you can see through my experiences, learning to forgive is a process.

All in all, we've acquired the knowledge as to the path we must take. Once you know your direction, steering the ship becomes easier. Then it's up to you to Navigate Your Existence.

RESTORE the Knowledge of the Ancestors

Chapter 6

New Age/Ancient Wisdom

So much truth lies in the age-old adage, "There's nothing new under the sun."

Humanity is experiencing a time when information is increasing rapidly: numerous new books being published; new discoveries in science, genetics, and technology; and New Age and New Thought movements arising. However, upon close examination, you will discover that this New Age information is actually ancient wisdom that was known to the indigenous people all over the world. In other words, this is old information that we are just rediscovering.

As we experience natural cycles of the universe, it is time for humanity to come into the knowing and the rediscovery of the natural laws of the universe. Much like sailing on the high seas, there are laws that affect our being. For instance, there are codes of conduct, laws of the sea, and a court system to balance or correct any infractions on the seas.

Admiralty Law deals with maritime questions and offenses, while the Law of the Sea defines the rights and responsibility of nations in the use of the oceans. In addition, we have Admiralty or Maritime

Courts to handle infractions. In much the same way, there are laws that exist within the universe that affect our very existence, whether we are cognizant of the fact or not.

As we continue to discover more about energy, and the physical (seen), and the metaphysical (unseen) world in which we live, we will grasp an increasingly profound understanding of our universe, its laws, and how they affect the vessel that is YOU!

The Universal Laws

The universe has provided a framework to guide our actions throughout our existence—a GPS or Global Positioning System of sorts, only on a universal level. The Universal Laws are designed as guidelines for acceptable and unacceptable behavior. The effects the Universal Laws have on you are determined by your actions.

The Universal Laws spring forth from the All, the One, the Source, the Creator. Therefore, the laws are exact. They do not discriminate; they do not care if you're Black or White, short or tall, rich or poor. Man cannot create laws; he establishes rules. Man proclaims rules, even if he calls them laws, which are subject to change for any number of given reasons. The Universal Laws are exact; they *never* change or waiver.

The concept of a universal law may seem new to some, but as we continue on, you will discover that you are already quite familiar with much of this information. For example, "What goes around comes around," and "Reap what you sow," are both based on Universal Law. So let's delve into the Universal Laws and examine more closely the framework established to guide our very existence.

Upon researching Universal Law, I encountered variations in the number of laws, their titles, and their definitions. That's interesting, especially since I just explicitly stated that the laws are exact.

Well, in actuality, there is only one law—the Law of One, (or the Law of Divine Oneness). Every other law and/or sub-law is an extension of the Law of One. The Law of One states that there is only the One, the All. Everything is connected and a part of the One. The explanation of any other law or sub-law will derive its definition from within the understanding of the Law of One.

Given the fact that these laws have been in existence since, "the beginning of time," might account for the various interpretations over the eons and across individual cultures. The oldest account of Universal Law, "The Seven Cosmic Principles," was recorded by the scribe Tehuti, from Kemet/Egypt, or even earlier from Atlantis. Later the Greeks adopted the principles into their philosophy. Tehuti became known by the Greeks as Thoth, and even later as Hermes. The Seven Principles presented by Tehuti became "The Seven Hermetic Principles."

My continued research led me to a version of Universal Law in which The Seven Cosmic Principles were extended into Twelve Universal Laws and twenty-two sub-laws. Although this version may seem over expanded, it tends to dissect the seven axioms into smaller, more easily understood concepts. With that intention in mind, during this journey we will explore the later interpretation. However, for the sake of brevity, we will only explore four Universal Laws.

Please view these descriptions of the Universal Laws as introductions. Further study of all the Universal Laws, including the varied accounts will lead to a more profound comprehension. With continued research, new and more penetrating discernment of each law will be realized. As we begin to explore the laws, you will see how they all overlap and emanate from the Divine essence of the One. As we move forward, you will continue to hear a consistent theme throughout the chapters, since *everything is connected*.

The Law of Divine Oneness

In order to comprehend The Law of Divine Oneness, we must fully understand that there is only Oneness, the One, the All. We must also comprehend that everything is Energy and that Energy is thought, or conscious. This Conscious Energy has been called *Prana, Chi, Ka, Life Force, God Source,* or *God*. All energy connects to form one Universal Mind, or one connected flow of consciousness.

Everything is comprised of thought (or energy), whether it be a rock, plant, animal, or whether it exists in the upper dimensions as spirit or etheric energy. Did you notice the connection to the seven dimensions? All dimensions share a universal mind of awareness or consciousness.

Just as our physical world is but an illusion of third-dimensional frequency and vibration, so too is our perception that everything is separate and functioning apart from the One. We are not separate.

What a person does or thinks will affect others. What others do or think affects you. No one and no thing escapes the encompassing, all-knowing conscious force of the One. A thought, word, or impulse sets this Conscious Energy into motion. "In the beginning, was the word...."

A major objective for the human condition is to reconnect *consciously* to the One.

The Law of Vibration

Everything in the universe is in perpetual motion, as all energy vibrates and travels in circular patterns. As you conceive a thought or utter a word, it vibrates and travels outwardly.

Think of a tuning fork or the bass tone coming through your stereo. Not only can you hear the sound, but you can feel its vibration passing through you on its way to its destination. Each thought, sound, or thing vibrates at its own speed or frequency. The slower the frequency, the slower the energy moves (the particles) and the thought manifests, or becomes visible or seen in our physical world. This relates to the previous discussion of *Solidified Thought*. Let's break this down a little deeper.

All of the physical items we perceive in our world began with an idea, a thought. That thought is pure conscious energy—that is, energy that is aware or knows what it is to be. Each word, idea, or thought has a frequency. As with all energy, it then begins to vibrate out into the world attracting to it particles. As the particles join together, or congeal, the result is that the item originally thought of manifests into reality. Or, in others words, the thought solidifies into matter. Thus the term *solidified thought*.

There…I hope that helps bring more concrete comprehension to these abstract concepts. Let's continue on.

Thoughts, or conscious energy, exist in the unseen world also. The faster the frequency and the faster the movement of the energy (particles), then the thought exists in the unseen realms or the metaphysical world. In other words, if the thought or conscious energy is vibrating so fast that the particles are so infinitesimal we cannot see them, that doesn't mean that the thought isn't there. In a like manner, in existence are the universal laws (or thoughts) that we can't see, but the laws affect us just the same.

Remember the "fan" on its highest setting? You can't see the blades, but you definitely feel the effects of the fan circulating at high speeds.

Subsequently, it is important to be cognizant of our thoughts, the words we speak or even allow in our realm. The more positive the word, the higher the vibration. Thus, the word *love* carries an extremely high vibration and allows your own vibration to increase. In contrast, negative words carry a low vibration. Accordingly, words like *hate* or *fear* cause your vibration to be lowered. Not only do the words we speak affect our vibrations, they affect the vibrations of the people around us.

Subsequently, the words others speak affect us as well. This is why, when you are surrounded by positive people, it tends to uplift your spirit. Of course, the converse is true, being around negative people, always spewing low-vibrational thoughts, words, and deeds, will drain your positive vibration and "bring you down."

The Law of Cause and Effect

The Law of Cause and Effect is one that many of us are familiar with on various levels. We've all heard that for every cause there will be an effect. When we drop a pebble into the lake (initiating a Cause), we will see ripples (creating an Effect).

Now let's take the Law of One and the Law of Vibration and apply them to the Law of Cause and Effect. Out of the Oneness comes the thought or word. The word vibrates according to the frequency of the word. Positive words have a higher or faster frequency, and negative words have a lower or slower frequency.

As the word, or energy of the word, travels outward and vibrates off particles, the particles begin to move according to the frequency (initiating cause) and start to take form or manifest, creating the reality (effect). As explained in the previous section, it is the vibration that sets the *cause* into motion. As the vibration bumps into particles, causing them to move or react, therein lies the *effect*.

Moving on, appreciation of the Law of Attraction will facilitate a more conclusive understanding of the previous laws. The Law of Attraction demonstrates how the laws overlap and work in unison; it helps to pull it all together so it begins to make sense.

The Law of Attraction

The Law of Attraction states that what you give attention to, you will attract into your life. Or, simply stated: "What you think about, you bring about."

All of the Universal Laws build on each other, so let's explore the Law of Attraction in relationship to the other laws. As previously covered, there is only One, the All. Everything is comprised of the One. Everything is connected. Everything is energy. With just a thought or a word, the One/Energy vibrates outwardly, causing an effect. The vibration will move particles (seen and unseen), causing them to arrange or manifest into reality (or that which is perceived as real).

Overall, reality for us on a third-dimensional realm is expressed in physical being, or that which we can actualize with our five senses. Reality can manifest in the form of an object, an emotion, or an event. If the thought or word projected was positive, the reality we experience is more of a positive nature. If our thoughts, words, or actions are negative, then our experiences we encounter will be more negative. Thus, we create our own reality!

We create this life that we are currently experiencing—yes, with all of its rewards, wonderful moments, and precious memories, as well as all of the pain, drama, hurt, and "why me?" moments.

As we begin to understand our universe and that energy exists everywhere and in all things, and as we learn the powers of the Universal Laws, we will discover that we are, in fact, co-creators of the universe. "In the Beginning was the Word…" If it is said that every being is made in the image of the One and the One has the power to create with thought or word, then so do we. You create your own reality. That which you see and experience in your life is but your own creation.

Now let's take another look at the creation powers you possess within.

Let's examine the Law of Attraction using the "magic lamp" analogy. What if you were given a magic lamp and told you could have anything your heart desired? All you had to do was ask the genie and rub the lamp. It seems just too good to be true. Well, what would this entail on your part?

Okay, first you would have to *think* about exactly what you wanted. Next, you would have to *ask* for what you wanted, *rub* the lamp, and—poof—your desired wish would *manifest* and appear right in front of your eyes. Wouldn't that be cool?

Let's look at this more closely from a different viewpoint utilizing the knowledge of the Universal Laws.

Step One: Think about what you want.	*Law of One* – Thought: the original impulse for energy in the *will* to move.
Step Two: Ask for what you want.	*Law of Vibration* – Speak the word, applying more vibration (positive/negative) to the thought.
Step Three: Action: Rub the lamp.	*Law of Cause and Effect* – You must take (cause) an action, resulting in an effect. Your thoughts will attract *like* energy to you. What you think about and act on will manifest. In our third-dimensional realm, manifestation will appear in the physical form of objects, emotion, and/or events.

So, in actuality, each of you already possesses your very own magic lamp, complete with the genie, all at your disposal to use to manifest your every desire. And it's free! However, it requires that you understand and practice the Law of Attraction.

Our thoughts, words, emotions, and actions cause energy to vibrate at a certain level. The higher the frequency, the more positive the energy; the lower the frequency, the more negative the energy. Our thoughts, words, emotions, and actions will attract like energy. Indeed, each of us creates our own reality. Each of us is responsible for the image we see in the mirror and for the conditions that affect our lives.

To illustrate the point, let's take a minute and talk about the word *manifest*. It took me years to understand the meaning of the term. Webster's defines *manifest* as: *apparent to the senses; to show plainly; reveal.* I always thought the ability to manifest was something only God could do.

Imagine the power to make something become real or to bring it into reality. Manifest means *to come into being*. We now know that we have the power to cause objects, emotions, and events to "come into being." Now we are able to conceptualize how the whole process works and why.

When you understand the Universal Laws, you fully grasp the concept of manifestation and internalize the notion that we create our own reality. Subsequently, we truly are responsible for what we manifest in our lives.

What a concept! I know…it really makes you think. It also makes you realize and admit that you are responsible for your life. No one has the power to control your being, your soul. If you do not like what you see or what is happening in your life, then change it! It really is that simple.

Unfortunately, simple is not always so easy. For many of us, it requires a major paradigm shift in our thinking. To utilize the Law of Attraction *effectively* to manifest our desires, we must first learn, understand, and believe the law. Then we must practice the law. I emphasize effectively, because the law is acting upon you (or you upon it) as we speak—whether or not we realize it or believe it. You have attracted everything in your current reality—the good, the bad, and the ugly.

Take RESPONSIBILITY RELEASE the Anchors

A Shift toward Taking Control

Taking control of your life's destination requires a shift in your mindset. For me, the introduction to the Universal Laws was a milestone in the transformation of my thinking like a victim. I say "introduction," because each time I read the laws I always seem to get yet a new deeper understanding. The idea that man can't make laws was eye-opening. The Universal Laws are exact; they exist and are available for our use to grant our deepest desires. A genie's lamp, at our disposal, and it's free.

With each new level of understanding, the feelings of powerlessness turn to powerfulness, and the feelings of being controlled transform into self-empowerment and control. As a result, I found a new sense of responsibility. Understanding that I am *both* responsible for what I've attracted into my life thus far and that I have the power to attract exactly what I desire into my life—is absolutely awesome!

Amazingly, with the act of taking *Responsibility* for our existence comes the awesome ability to *Release the Anchors. Knowing* it is my actions, thoughts and deeds that create my reality requires that I stop blaming others for what ails me in this life. To further drive home the onus of taking responsibility for the life you've created requires delving into the subject of karma and revisiting the discussion of reincarnation.

Karma and Reincarnation

Having analyzed four of the Universal Laws affords us the opportunity to comprehend the concepts Karma and Reincarnation at a deeper level. Possessing an awareness of the Universal Laws and how they work, affords one the ability to understand why each individual is responsible for his/her actions.

The concept of karma has been receiving much attention lately and begs for some discussion. Although karma and reincarnation are fairly new concepts in the Western world, they have been a part of Eastern and indigenous cultures for eons.

Karma is a product (or aspect of) the Law of Cause and Effect and is often misunderstood. The concept of karma is known to many of us through our familiarity with the saying, "What goes around, comes around." Karma, in its most simplistic explanation, means that according to your actions, you will be the recipient of the *effect* of that which you *caused*.

As previously stated, all actions or thoughts have a vibrational energy or frequency. As that frequency travels in a circular motion, what you set into motion (cause) will return and have a corresponding (effect) on you. "As you sow, so shall you reap" is yet another adage that speaks to the Law of Cause and Effect, and the concept of karma.

Many people think of karma as a system of rewards and punishments according to their actions. That is a distortion of sorts. Remember, the laws are exact…they do not discriminate. The response you receive is in accordance to how you acted upon the law.

Let me give you an example.

I learned the Law of Cause and Effect and the aspect of karma at an early age. At the time, I had no knowledge of the term *karma*, its meaning or its effects. I was attending a new junior high school and had acquired new friends. They were playing jokes on each other saying, "Excuse me, you dropped something," causing the person to stop and look around when nothing had been dropped. While the person was searching, everyone would begin laughing and the person would soon realize he or she was the recipient of a prank.

Well, against my better judgment, I joined in with this misbehavior. It is said that when you reap what you've sown, the corresponding effect (be it positive or negative) is felt to a higher or more intense degree.

One day my mother called and instructed me to meet her at her job. Now when my mother told me to meet her at work, I knew I had better be appropriately dressed, well groomed, and on time! As I was rushing down the street, trying to make it to the train that would get me to my mother's job right at 5:30 p.m., a grown man called out to me. "Hey, little girl; look, you dropped something." I stopped and looked all around, but I didn't see anything.

I looked up at the stranger and he was smiling at me. Realizing I hadn't dropped anything, I turned around and hurried to the subway more afraid than ever that I was going to miss my train. Thank goodness, I made it to the train on time. During the ride, I sat there trying to assess what had just transpired and why?

Okay, I knew and understood the adage "What goes around comes around." Yet I couldn't help but wonder…What would make a grown man want to take the time to play a prank—and on a complete stranger? My school was not located near my home, so it's unlikely that he witnessed me in the act of playing pranks on my friends.

I wondered about this incident for years. Maybe it was the universe's way of teaching me the Law of Cause and Effect, karma—at an early age. The lesson could not have come at a worst time. It caused me a great deal of anxiety and would have resulted in grave consequences had I missed my train. I would have had to experience the wrath of my mother.

Boy, did I get the message and a lesson learned for life! And I had the benefit of learning a lesson at an early age that affected my future choices.

In as much as this is just a simple example demonstrating how karma works, it served a purpose and taught me an important lesson. It did cause me some anxious moments, fortunately, it was not a negative life-altering event. In order to understand karma and its implications on a more profound level, we need to revisit the earlier discussion on reincarnation.

Reincarnation is also an aspect of the Law of Cause and Effect in that it relates to karma and the opportunity to alter karmic deeds.

Do you remember how I became acquainted with the book, *"Life After Life"* on that fateful day when the lights went out? That was my initial introduction to reincarnation, and it afforded me a basic overall understanding. Yet, it precluded any knowledge of the Universal Laws, and I hadn't yet acquired a thorough grasp on the concept of energy.

Reincarnation is the philosophical belief that when you "die," at some point in the future you return to the Earth with the opportunity to change your karmic balance sheet, if you will. In other words, you have an opportunity to do a "good" deed to pay off or balance a "negative" deed you have on your account from a previous life. Or you have an opportunity to "learn the lesson" you didn't grasp in the previous life. The idea is that as you clear your Akashic Record, you raise your vibration, allowing access to a higher position in the dimensions the next time you "die" or transition. Think of it as learning your lessons, or doing your homework so you can graduate.

With my new point of reference, understanding Universal Law and the world of energy, it affords a more profound comprehension of the relationship between karma and reincarnation.

With this intention in mind, let's review some of the concepts we've covered.

We now understand that when you "die," the energy within doesn't die; it transitions to another realm or dimension. The essence that is you, your memories, your experiences, and your soul continue on.

Universal Law responds to what you think, say or do. Your thoughts, actions, and deeds will vibrate outward, causing an effect. All actions are recorded in an invisible "book" called the Akashic Records. In actuality, the Akashic Records are merely a representation of all thoughts, actions, and deeds recorded in the energetic field of life. All energy travels in circles. What you set into motion (cause) will eventually return and have an (effect) upon you. If what you cause by your actions, thoughts, and deeds are positive and vibrate at a high frequency, then you will be the recipient of positive effects. And of course the converse is also true.

Eventually your soul, or the energy that in essence is you, will have an opportunity to return to this realm, the Earth, with your record of deeds. Upon your return, you have an opportunity to balance your record sheet. This is your chance to learn lessons from your missteps in your last life. In order to learn the lesson, challenges or tests will be presented to you. How well you react to the challenge determines if you will have to experience the lesson again. So, issues that challenge us or cause us stress are not for the purpose of punishment. In contrast, the challenges present the possibility to clear our slates, balance the records, or clear our karmic history.

A Long Look in the Mirror

This brings us back to the realization that you alone are responsible for what you've manifested in your life, be it this lifetime or another. Consequently, it is you and you alone who has the responsibility and the power to change that which does not suit you. Taking responsibility for your life is a huge undertaking. It requires a lot of self-reflection. It requires that we take "a long look in the mirror."

Taking responsibility demands that you release the limiting beliefs and replace them with a belief system that dictates your power to accomplish anything you will. Taking responsibility necessitates relinquishing the victim mentality and regaining control over your life. Stated more emphatically, taking responsibility and releasing the anchors results in your transition from victim to victor.

On that note, I would also like to share with you an example from my own journey to demonstrate how taking responsibility leads to greater self-empowerment.

Personal Self-Reflection

Talk about self-reflection and taking responsibility! To illustrate the point, please allow me to share some integral aspects of marriage Number Two. Twelve long years had passed since my first marriage ended in divorce, and if there was ever to be another husband, certain prerequisites were in order. In other words, I had a list! In short, I had a sheet of paper, folded into three columns and filled with criteria, or "Must-Haves." Determined not to settle, I spent long hours contemplating the traits and characteristics I desired in a man. Additionally, I certainly had no desire to repeat the problems of my first marriage.

Then one day, when I wasn't even looking…I met him! I was in heaven; I had met my Mr. Right. In all honesty, he didn't meet all of the criteria on my long list, but he came pretty close. Of course, just like all relationships, it started out like a dream. We were only together for one year before we got married. Life was great and I was happy.

After a couple of years, things started to go downhill. As the years progressed, the downhill trek seemed to pick up speed. At one point, it seemed as if my husband was apologizing about something on a regular basis. Subsequently, he began to say, "I know I messed up and I apologize for it, but you never apologize for anything. You never admit that you've done anything wrong."

To this I replied, "That's because I don't do anything to you! I do everything in my power to be a good wife. I support you in every way I know how; I do everything and anything I can fathom to make this marriage work." I honestly felt that I was trying my best to be a good wife, good friend, and a good person. I could not see where I was at fault and needed to apologize for anything.

Ultimately, we found ourselves at the point of no return, where far too many couples arrive. Now things were at the bottom of the hill, with nowhere else to go.

One day I remember thinking to myself, "He is starting to act just like my first husband." Hmmm…Then one day, I glanced at him and he *looked* just like my first husband. I mean physically—facial characteristics and everything. Case in point: when I got married, my husband did not resemble or act in any way similar to my first husband. Well, there could only be one explanation, and the realization struck me like lightning. The only connection between the two of them was ME. It MUST be something I'M doing. Wow! Now all I had to do was figure out what on Earth I was doing to cause this transformation. Yes, it was time to take "a long look in the mirror!"

No matter how hard I tried to ascertain the part I was playing in the demise of my marriage, the answer escaped me. It would be years later before the answer surfaced, but by that time, I was divorced. So you want to know what I discovered? Without getting into too much detail, here is the simplified explanation.

The truth is that my initial breakthrough originated during a conference where the renowned Roy Masters, founder of the Foundation of Human Understanding, was speaking. Master's insights, coupled with some deep introspection, led me to the following conclusions.

The behavior or actions on my part that led to difficulty in both marriages originated in my youth. It all stemmed from a childhood without loving relationships. My need to be loved and my desire to keep my family together are so important to me that I tend to overextend myself in relationships. This causes an imbalance in the give and take in the relationship, (giving too much, and expecting too little, and accepting anything). Furthermore, it creates a sense of loss of power, loss of respect, and being taken for granted in my relationships. Along with that comes a feeling of resentment. I could go on from there, but you get the gist of things. So, in actuality, I *was* doing something wrong. And I have no doubt my ex-husband could add a number things on my part for which he felt an apology was in order.

Even when I wanted to blame my husband for the condition of our relationship, ultimately I had to take responsibility for my part in shaping the construct. Again, when you relinquish your power, you lose your control, and then you open yourself up to become a victim. And the blame game begins.

Whatever situation, scenario, and/or event that shows up in your life, take responsibility! Dig deep and find out why it's at your door. What part did you play in attracting it, and what is the lesson? Stop attempting to blame the other person, or fix the other person, and look deep within. Even if you cannot figure out why or what it is you're doing to attract the situation, once you understand Universal Laws, the onus is upon you to accept the responsibility and keep working at it until you understand the part you play. You and only you are responsible for your life, and you and only you can change it!

Universal Laws and Sub-Laws

Now that we have learned that important lesson, let's move on to providing you with a comprehensive summary of the Universal Laws to wrap up this chapter and put everything in perspective for your own journey.

In *The Light Shall Set You Free* (Athena Publishing, Scottsdale, AZ, 1996), authors Dr. Norma J. Milanovich and Dr. Shirley D. McCune contend there are twelve Universal Laws and twenty-one sub-laws. The Universal Laws can be viewed as guidelines for behaviors that will enhance our physical, mental, emotional, and spiritual growth. The sub-laws are ways in which to put the Universal Laws into action.

The Universal Laws are all interrelated and founded on the understanding that everything in the universe is energy, including us, and that energy moves in a circular fashion. At the microscopic level, we are a whirling mass of rapidly spinning atoms. In fact, everything in the world is comprised of energy and we are intimately connected with this sea of energy and whirling atoms.

Our thoughts, feelings, words, and actions are all forms of energy. What we think, feel, say, and do in each moment comes back to us to create our realities. Energy moves in a circle, so what goes around comes around. The combined thoughts, feelings, words, and actions of everyone on the planet create our collective consciousness and the world we see before us.

The exciting news is that this dynamic gives us the power to create a world of peace, harmony, and abundance. In order to do this, it is essential that we learn to control our thoughts and emotions. Understanding the Universal Laws is the secret, so let's take a closer look at them.

Here is a summary of these laws excerpted from *The Light Shall Set You Free:*

1. The Law of Divine Oneness

Divine Oneness helps us to understand that we live in a world where all things are connected to each other. Everything we do, say, think, and believe affects others and the universe around us.

2. The Law of Vibration

This law states that everything in the universe moves, vibrates, and travels in circular patterns. The same principles of vibration in the physical world apply to our thoughts, feelings, desires, and wills in the etheric world. Each sound, thing, and even thought has its own vibrational frequency, unique unto itself.

3. The Law of Action

The Law of Action must be applied in order for us to manifest things on Earth. Therefore, we must engage in actions that support our thoughts, dreams, emotions, and words.

4. The Law of Correspondence

The principles or laws of physics that explain the physical world – energy, light, vibration, and motion – have their corresponding principles in the etheric world or universe. "As Above, So Below."

5. The Law of Cause and Effect

This law states that nothing happens by chance or outside the Universal Laws. Every action has a reaction or consequence and we "reap what we have sown."

6. The Law of Compensation

This is the Law of Cause and Effect applied to blessings and abundance that are provided for us. The visible effects of our deeds are given to us in gifts, money, inheritances, friendships, and blessings.

7. The Law of Attraction

This law demonstrates how we create the things, events, and people that come into our lives. Our thoughts, feelings, words, and actions produce energies that, in turn, attract like energies. Negative energies attract negative energies, and positive energies attract positive energies.

8. The Law of Perpetual Transmutation of Energy

This law states that all persons have within them the power to change the conditions in their lives. Higher vibrations consume and transform lower ones; thus, each of us can change the energies in our lives by understanding the Universal Laws and applying the principles in such a way as to effect change.

9. The Law of Relativity

This law states that each person will receive a series of problems (Tests of Initiation) for the purpose of strengthening the Light within. We must consider each of these tests to be a challenge and remain connected to our hearts when proceeding to solve the problems. This law also teaches us to compare our problems to that of others' and put everything into its proper perspective. No matter how bad we perceive our situation to be, there is always someone who is in a worse position. It is all relative.

10. The Law of Polarity

This law states that everything is on a continuum and has an opposite. We can suppress and transform undesirable thoughts by concentrating on the opposite pole. It is the Law of Mental Vibrations.

11. The Law of Rhythm

This law states that everything vibrates and moves to certain rhythms that establish seasons, cycles, stages of development, and patterns. Each cycle reflects the regularity of God's universe. Masters know how to rise above negative parts of a cycle by never getting too excited or allowing negative things to penetrate their consciousness.

12. The Law of Gender

This law states that everything has its masculine (yang) and feminine (yin) principles, and that these are the basis for all creation. The spiritual initiate must balance the masculine and feminine energies within herself or himself to become a Master and a true co-creator with God.

Sub-laws

In addition to the twelve Universal Laws, Drs. Milanovich and McCune state that there are twenty-one sub-laws of the universe that are governed by the Higher Self.

The twenty-one sub-laws actually represent human characteristics that relate to the Universal Laws. These characteristics are: Aspiration to A Higher Power, Charity, Compassion, Courage, Dedication, Faith, Forgiveness, Generosity, Grace, Honesty, Hope, Joy, Kindness, Leadership, Non-interference, Patience, Praise, Responsibility, Self-Love, Thankfulness, and Unconditional Love.

Incorporating the Universal Laws into your journey is such a monumental milestone on your journey to resurrection. Each time I revisited this information afforded me yet a deeper understanding of the profound, esoteric meaning, enabling me to translate it further into my current reality. And so it will be for you too as you continue on your voyage to Navigate Your Existence, utilizing these laws to empower yourself. See the Action Steps below for ways you can apply the laws to your everyday life.

CATCH THE WAVE – *Chapter Summary*

IMPORTANT POINTS TO REMEMBER
- Universal Laws spring forth from the One, the Source, the Creator.
- Man cannot make Universal Laws. Man can make rules and call them laws, but Universal Laws come from the Creator.
- Universal Laws provide a framework for our behavior. They respond to our actions accordingly whether or not we are cognizant of that fact.
- Karma is not a system of rewards and punishments, but one based on the Universal Law of Cause and Effect. We reap what we sow. Positive behavior recycles positive reaction. Negative behavior generates negative response.
- The Akashic Records is a virtual accounting system recording our every deed. Think of it as a universal balance sheet.
- You create your own reality. Based on the Law of Attraction, you are responsible for what you manifest in your life. If you don't like what you see, then you have the power to change it.

ACTION STEPS
- Take the time to really study and understand the Universal Laws. Each law is profound in and of itself, and the longer you study, the more penetrating your level of understanding.
- Pay attention to your every deed. Make a conscious effort to put forth positive energy in your actions. The more positive energy you send out, the more you receive…and the more positive vibrations will circulate our planet.
- Shift your mentality from victim to victor. Understand the totality of the concept that you have the power.

- Take Responsibility for your life:
  - Make a list of everything that is going well. Congratulate yourself, because you attracted these positive events.
  - Make a list of the things that are not going well in your life. Be very careful not to blame anyone for these events. Take responsibility and realize that you attracted these events. Now create a list of exactly what you must do to change each situation. And…JUST DO IT!
- Respect the power of the word. Work on rephrasing your thoughts and words. Refrain from using negative, low-vibrational words. Do not select words that dictate limitations, remembering that *you can do anything*! For example:

Change:	To:
I hate this rainy weather.	I'd prefer a sunny day to all of this rain.
I can never seem to get this right.	I will work at this until it meets my satisfaction
I wish I could…	I Have…I Am

- Take the word *TRY* out of your vocabulary. Either you will or you won't. You have the power. If it is something you want to do, get it done!
- Perform Random Acts of Kindness— just because!

LIFE LESSONS FOR TRANSFORMATION

Man cannot make Universal Laws. Man can only make rules, call them laws, and then change them at his discretion.

When I became aware of this concept, it hit me like a rock. There are so many rules and "laws" in society, many of which we are afraid to break for fear of repercussions from the controlling forces. There is a saying, "The one who has the gold makes the rules." In other words, those who control the money get to make the rules. Since they are in control, they also get to enforce the rules and change them at will.

Understanding the Universal Laws, how they work, and incorporating that knowledge into your world is truly life-changing. Once you really comprehend that absolutely no one has control over you, you experience a true sense of freedom. For me, it was one the most liberating moments of my life.

Now don't get me wrong. Certainly societies need rules and regulations to keep things running smoothly. I am not suggesting that you wake up tomorrow and throw all the rules out of the window, or go up to the mountain and live outside of societal norms. "When in Rome, do as the Romans do." That doesn't mean you have to BE a Roman.

However, now that you know the difference between rules and laws, the word *emancipation* takes on a different connotation. Emancipation from slavery was just one step toward my freedom. Now I feel like I have the knowledge to be emancipated from society's "Box" and can go on to become a citizen of the universe.

At this point, you might be thinking that all of this *sounds* good, yet wondering how it *shows up* in real life. Many of you may be contemplating real-life scenarios, for example…I still have to pay taxes and follow the "rules." Yes, at some level we still have to function within the confines of society, but society doesn't have to own your soul. You belong to a bigger "society," a universal society. Once you realize that you can utilize the Law of Attraction to manifest change in your life, then your life will change.

On to the Next Port of Call

As we have completed the first leg of our journey to Chart the Course, let's pause for a moment to take stock before moving on to the next port of call. We have learned about energy, metaphysics, the Universal Laws, and the wisdom of the ancients and how this applies to our modern world. But how does this address the resurrection of the African American?

This is your story! The essence of this knowledge is locked deep within your very core. These are the secrets of the ancestors, and it is time to *Recognize* what's holding you back. Time to *Restore* the knowledge that created a once great race of people. But in order to do such, it is so important to pay special attention to the keys RESPONSIBILITY and RELEASE, Take Responsibility, and Release the Anchors. Please allow me to expound.

As I learned about energy, I had to look at all of the issues that plague African Americans from another perspective. It did not cause the issues to change at all, because they are real and very present in our lives. However, the perspective in which I viewed the issues and dealt with them changed greatly.

Upon my introduction to the Universal Laws, one of the aspects that really impressed me was that the laws are *exact*! They do not waiver under any condition. They do not discriminate.

If in fact you believe in the Universal Laws and you take a look at the condition of the African American today, the issue of karma and karmic debt should come to mind. Now that's deep, and I'm sure that some will not want to or are not ready to deal with this concept. The Law of Karma says, "What goes around comes around," in other words, you receive the effect of the cause you put out. Well, this brings some questions to the forefront.

What did we do to deserve this treatment? Or, are we responsible for this treatment and we're just getting what we deserve? What? Are we responsible for slavery?

Well, the answers are no and yes.

No, we didn't physically knock ourselves over the head, place chains around our necks and feet, and jump on the slave ship. And, yes, the law of karma is exact.

People or groups of people have karma just as an individual has a karma, or karmic balance sheet. I will not attempt to identify what karmic debt or action we are balancing. Although some say it had to do with falling out of alignment with Universal Law. But, can we talk?

Let's get real. Until we understand the laws of energy and learn to utilize them, *we cannot heal.* We cannot become empowered functioning in the habits of blame and anger. We must understand the law and take responsibility for the karmic debt *and* take responsibility to change the situation.

I cannot express to you how empowering this lesson was for me. When you *truly* understand Universal Law, and you *truly* understand how powerful you are, you will no longer have the time to sit in any situation that is not conducive to your higher being. You will no longer have the time or the desire to point fingers or blame anyone for what has been "done" to you. Release the baggage; release the blame and anger. It only serves to rob you of valuable energy you could be using to manifest the life you desire and deserve. Utilize that energy to change your condition. You are a magnificent being. You are co-creator of the universe. The time is now for you to rise.

Now, with that said, let's move on to the next port of call and Start the Engines.

Part Two

Start The Engines
Preparation for Optimal Performance

The Scarab Beetle
Kemetic/Egyptian Symbol of Resurrection

Start the Engines

Preparation for Optimal Performance

Introduction

We began this journey by asking a series of questions

- Who's conducting the ship?
- What's the ship's destination?
- In which direction must it travel to get there?
- Is the ship prepared for the journey? Is it cleaned, oiled, and fueled?
- Has the course been charted?

So far, we have covered volumes of information and acquired an abundance of knowledge to utilize in preparation for the journey.

Who's conducting *your* ship? Are you in control or is someone else at the helm? Is it your boss, your spouse, or your pastor? Are you still complying with the societal norms set up for us by the various institutions?

As our world transitions through these evolutionary times, so too must humanity find its evolutionary path. As we continue to discover new information, that which we consider true gives way to the new discoveries and makes way for the new "truth" of the day.

Remaining stuck in a mindset, just because it worked for us in the past, is no longer an option. It is time to raise our consciousness to a higher understanding and take control of our destiny. *You* must be the conductor of your ship. The energy that is you, and resides within you, will determine your path. *You* must be at the helm; *you* must control the rudder; and ultimately it is *you* who must control your direction.

What's your destination? Most would agree that our ultimate destination is UP! Understanding dimensions and our physical and metaphysical worlds affords a more comprehensive view of ascension. Yes, I certainly want my ship heading upward, one dimension (level) at a time; however, a hyper-jump straight to the top would work for me just fine.

Do you have a plan? Have you charted your course? The nautical charts are already designed for you. The entire universal GPS is graphed, plotted, and available for your use.

The Universal Laws provide the grand design with the guidelines and framework for humanity to utilize. Remember: the Universal Laws are exact. How you choose to act upon these laws will determine your direction, resulting in a sojourn upward (ascension), or downward ("descension").

A "descension," or downward trek, mandates the repercussion of remaining within the physical realms of the first three dimensions. I don't know about you, but given the information presented, my course of action includes ascension to the Fifth Dimension!

This leads us right into Step Two of our preparation. Now we need to give some time and attention to the preparation of our ship for optimal performance. Getting our vessel in tip-top shape and pristine condition requires that we look within, or "inside-out." Such a process requires that:

- We examine or inspect our vessel down to the smallest detail
- We swab the deck and clean our ship for travel

- We oil and fuel our engines, making sure to utilize not only the correct fuel, but premium grade
- We…Start the Engines!

Now that we know we have some work to do, let's explore how to prepare the ship—the vessel that is You. We will begin by examining the vessel we have in our possession. It's time to get out the magnifying glass as we begin the process of inspecting our vessel down to the most minute detail…to get out the microscope as we examine the tiniest speck…leaving nothing to chance, preparing our vessel for optimal performance from the inside out.

Yet, delving into this next section requires that we step back and clear some waves for smooth sailing through this next topic.

ASCENSION/DESCENSION

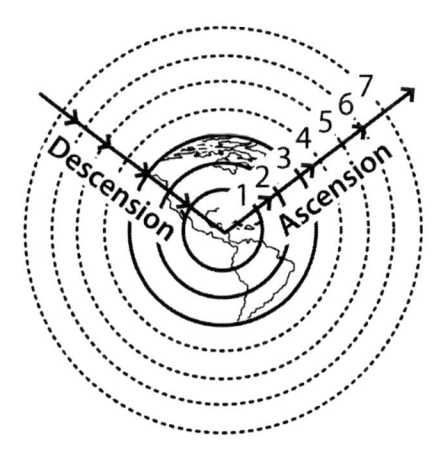

↗ Ascension
- A Rise in Consciousness/Awareness
- Aware of the Law of One
- Cognizant the All and Everything is Connected

↘ Descension
- A Fall in Consciousness/Awareness
- Lack of Awareness of the Law of One
- Existing in a Reality based on Separateness and Individuality

Out of the One Come Many

This means that we are all from Source energy, all created in the likeness of God...Energy/Thought! Be we Black or White, tall or short, born with four limbs or none, in our totality we share in the one universal mind. We all have the ability to create our own reality. No matter what level we perceive ourselves to be separate or independent, there is but one universal mind. With that said, this leads us perfectly into our next discussion on melanin.

As we reincarnate to this third-dimensional realm, each of us chooses the body with which to navigate this life's existence. We are spiritual beings experiencing an earthly reality. We select the body that will allow us to learn the lessons we need to actualize in this incarnation. And, YES, there are differences: in appearances and in lessons to learn, as well as physiological characteristics.

However, if one truly comprehends the concept of the Law of One, then the discussion of superiority or inferiority becomes a moot point. Each of us possesses exactly that which we need to facilitate the experience necessary for this life's journey.

As we surge forward into this next very sensitive topic, please remember that ultimately THERE IS ONLY THE ONE, and from the ONE comes the ALL. We are all extensions of the One, the universal mind. We are co-creators of our world, and we are all connected. We are responsible for our actions and responsible to each other because of our connectedness; what one does will affect the other. Am I my brother's keeper? Yes, I am!

REACTIVATE Your Energy Sources

Chapter 7

Melanin, Energy, and You

As we continue our journey inward, examining the powers *within,* it is time to investigate energy at a biological, molecular level. That brings us to the profound discussion of melanin. What is it? And what does it do?

If you asked someone those questions, the common response would be that melanin is *something* in the skin that protects us from the ultraviolet rays of the sun and determines our skin color. That's very similar to the answer I received many years ago as a young girl.

Yes, that same little girl who always had questions, now wanted to know more. I remember that day when I marched into the kitchen and asked, "Mommy, why am I Black?" Of course, the question arose from living in a predominantly White society, being told that I was a minority, and being treated as a second-class citizen. Being teased because of my skin color and tightly curled hair and feeling out of place also triggered the inquiry.

The answer I received—"because we have pigment in our skin"—didn't sufficiently answer my question. It was the '60s and there had not been a lot of discussion in the mainstream about melanin.

I wondered, "What is pigment, anyway?" It sounded too much like "pig" to me, so I had no inclination to investigate the term further. I just pushed the question to the back of my mind, just as my mother taught me to do. It was not until many years later, in 1990, while attending a melanin conference sponsored by Black scientists and scholars that I began to receive some answers.

Consequently, during the three-day event, I was introduced to the fascinating phenomenon of melanin. I discovered that melanin had been the subject of extensive research since as early as 1658. Numerous studies have been conducted on the melanocyte, the cell that produces melanin. As a matter of fact, the melanocyte is the third most studied cell in the world, only surpassed by the red blood cell and the nerve cell.

Over the years the research has increased and so too have the volumes of information available on the subject. For instance, I discovered that in the 1990s, annual melanin conferences were hosted by European countries for European scientists. Moreover, Harvard reserves a section in its medical library specifically for melanin and its study. It was amazing to me that such extensive research existed on the subject, yet the public knew little to nothing on the topic. Even our ancestors were intuitively well aware of melanin, its properties, and its powers, yet the present-day masses are ignorant of the phenomenon that is melanin.

Before I delve further into the subject, let me affirm that I am not a scientist—at least not in the traditional sense of the word. For me to attempt a thorough explanation of melanin would be a discredit to the many scientists and scholars who have spent years of research on the subject.

There have been numerous studies resulting in scientific evidence documenting melanin's functions and physiological as well as psychological implications for the body, mind, and spirit. So I implore you to exercise due diligence and research this important subject for yourself. For the purpose of this discussion, I will provide an overview of some of my research and findings on the subject and why it represents a vital part of our journey.

THE MELANIN MOLECULE

Free, Clean, Renewable Energy…Melanin is the Chemical Key to Life!!

Melanin: What Is It?

In addition to melanin being an absolutely fascinating phenomenon, it is defined by its distinctive characteristics.

"Melanin is a biochemical substance that drives physical, mental, emotional and spiritual life." Llaila Afrika (2009).

Melanin is a black molecule with physical and chemical properties. It is present in different parts of the body; i.e., skin, organs, the brain, and the glands. In the skin, melanin is a hormone released from specialized cells called melanocytes. Melanin is also produced in the pineal gland and excreted as the hormones melatonin and serotonin.

The word itself means *black*, derived from the stem *khem in khemistry/chemistry* which is the study of matter (or dark matter – melanin),

Khem in Kemet/ Egypt, which means black, and later from the Greek word melano, which means black. Why is it black? *"MELANIN is BLACK simply because of its chemical composition that will not allow any type of energy to escape once energy has come into contact with its structure."* (Carol Barnes 1988) All life must have melanin to exist. Melanin is present in soil, plants, animals, and in the human fetus at conception. *Everyone* has melanin, although each individual's genetics determines the capacity to produce melanin, the type of melanin produced, and his/her ability to interact with the external environment.

Melanin is key and central to existence, and it's a physical manifestation of our universe. This means that the melanin that exists in our third-dimensional realm is a replica of the dark matter that exists in the universe. Better yet, melanin is the stuff that fills the space between the stars. So scientists are now discovering that what we perceive to be empty space is not empty at all.

Wow! This is already fascinating! Now the question becomes "What are the implications for the mind, body, and soul?"

Melanin: What Does It Do?

First, let's explore the commonly accepted concept that melanin protects us from the sun.

Here's an excerpt from T. Owens Moore, PhD, in his book *Dark Matters, Dark Secrets* (Zamani Press, ©2002):

The advances made in the area of melanin research have led to numerous hypotheses and postulations about the extra-pigmentary effects of melanin. Melanin is commonly known as the pigment on the external surface of the body, which provides protection from the sun's harmful ultraviolet radiation.

However, the use of modern scientific technology has generated an interest in the bio-electronic properties of melanin. Our nervous system is dependent upon electrochemical communication for normal behavioral functioning to occur.

So the electrical properties of dark matter (melanin) are critical for normal behavior to be expressed in organisms with complex nervous systems. Conversely, the absence of external and/or internal melanin can greatly diminish life.

So, yes, melanin protects us from the harmful, toxic rays of the sun and contributes to the determination of skin, hair, and eye color. Yet, we have discovered that melanin does so much more! For instance, some of the benefits of melanin include:

- Memory Enhancement
- Cancer Prevention
- Antioxidant Properties
- Boosts the Immune System
- Anti-Aging and Anti-Wrinkling Qualities

Furthermore, melanin is connected to the nervous system and enhances rhythm and balance. It is melanin that allows Michael Jordan to fly through the air and explains why LeBron James has hang time. Of course I am referring to the awesome basketball skills displayed by both men. This is the effect of melanin at work in their nervous systems. It's what gives you that *swag* in your step, that rhythm we call *soul*.

But there's more. Melanin is also a conductor of energy. It acts like a battery collecting and storing energy from the sun and our environment, then utilizes that energy to enhance mental, physical, and spiritual performance. Sunlight increases the production of melanin in the skin.

Remember our discussion of energy and how all energy travels in circles? Well it is melanin in our natural nappy hair that causes our hair to grow in circles, spiraling up to the sun—acting like antennae, drawing God Source energy back into our bodies. Understanding this truth should cause you to celebrate your natural nappy hair.

Melanin is connected to our five senses, enhancing sensory perception of our external environment. This aids in intuition. When we have a "feeling" about something, it is melanin at work. When we sense someone behind us, it's melanin. When the hair stands up on the back of the neck, it's melanin. Melanin connects the internal energy with the external energy in our environment.

Moore further explains melanin's phenomenal properties as such:

In terms of external stimuli, light is not just the color sensation perceived by the eye; light is also heat, radiation, laser waves, cosmic waves, radio waves, TV waves, magnetism, and electrical currents. Due to melanin's tremendous capacity to absorb these forms of light and use them as energy sources to recharge itself and the cells in which it is located, melanin's strategic relationship with the central nervous system also gives us the capacity to immediately know what is happening to us within our external environment. This gives human beings great ability to be aware of their internal environment and constantly be recharged and regenerated from interacting with the external environment.

Melanin connects our internal energy (spirit) to Mother Nature, the universal mind, Divine Consciousness—or external Energy. Energy is the All and it is aware or conscious. Thus, melanin connects us to the Life Force or Source Energy, or God Consciousness. Amazing! Are you getting this? Isn't this knowledge powerful?

Melanin, Race, and the Color Issue

Albeit, as powerful as this information regarding melanin is, I feel compelled to take a moment and bring this discussion down to a very basic, earthly, third-dimensional level. Over the course of the last six chapters, we discussed energy, Universal Laws, how energy is connected to the ALL, and that we are all from the same source. And, yes, I stand by my every word. The research and discoveries regarding melanin do not preclude the Law of One: that everything and everyone ultimately emanates from source energy.

However, given the aforementioned information, it appears that melanin affords a certain quality of life to melanin-dominant persons. This information about melanin is based on scientific research and documented by masters in various fields of science. Why, then, do people become nervous when we talk about melanin? It is because of our socialization, institutionalization, and "mis-education" that causes us to feel uncomfortable.

For instance, many would say in response to the aforementioned information on melanin that it's "reverse racism." To say that there is a chemical that aids in mental, spiritual, emotional, and physical enhancement—that is predominant in one group of people as opposed to another "suggests racism"—begs for further discussion.

First of all, we must ascertain a clear understanding of the term *racism*. It is a term that is commonly used and just as commonly used incorrectly. As defined by *Collins English Dictionary* (Complete & Unabridged 10th Edition, 2009 © William Collins Sons & Co. Ltd. © HarperCollins Publishers, 2009), *racism* is: "a belief or doctrine that inherent differences among the various human races determine cultural or individual achievement, usually involving the idea that one's own race is superior and has the right to rule others."

Our current structure of racism is based on the belief in white supremacy, out of which evolved a system of control by White people over the non-White people of the world. An inherent aspect of racism is the perceived *"right"* to control others based on the precept of superiority. Therefore, unless a group or race is in the position to control another group, that race cannot be classified as racist. That being said, it does not detract or make less relevant the information concerning melanin. Nor does it provide any validation to the notion of reverse racism.

A noted psychiatrist, Frances Cress Welsing, MD, provides an excellent dissertation on the topics of race, racism, and white supremacy in her book entitled, *THE ISIS PAPERS – The Keys to the Colors* (Third World Press, Chicago, © 1991). I encourage you to familiarize yourself with her work. As a matter of fact, it should be required reading for anyone who wants to engage in a discourse on white supremacy and racism.

The system of racism as it exists today is based on the engineered separation of the human race into sub-categories, in which a people claim superiority solely for the purpose of domination over other peoples of the world. So again, unless you are in the position to control another "race" or group of people, there can be no reverse racism.

The Color Complex

The discussion of melanin is no doubt going to stir some dialogue from within the ranks of the Black community as well. One would think that the information on melanin would be openly welcomed. However, given our history with issues regarding race and color, any such topic will require deep and emotional reflection. So let's look at color issues, or the color complex, within the Black community.

The term *color complex* refers to the complicated issue of variations of skin color, and the benefits and disadvantages associated accordingly.

The systems of white supremacy, slavery, and race discrimination generated a culture in which the lighter-skinned Black people were favored over those with darker skin. This practice continues until this very day as we witness lighter-skinned Black people "awarded" social perks, such as better opportunities in jobs, education, and social status.

In turn, we African Americans picked up the same mentality and also began to favor lighter skin and to dislike our dark skin. The system resulted in lighter-skinned people getting ahead in society, which in turn further fueled the preference of light skin within the Black community. It is a socialization process that continues today, causing African Americans to reject the natural melanin or dark pigmentation of our own skin. Furthermore, we even bought into the color discourse to the extent of reciting chants denoting the level of our acceptability based on the tone of our skin.

If you are white, you're all right,
If you are yellow, you are mellow,
If you are brown, stick around,
If you are black, get back!

A book that deals with this topic is *The Color Complex: The Politics of Skin Color among African Americans* by Kathy Russell, Midge Wilson, Ph.D., and Ronald Hall.

Here is an excerpt from that book discussing the matter in detail:

While many prefer not to discuss it, especially in the company of Whites, others contend that skin color bias no longer exists—that it's history, water under the bridge. Yet beneath a surface appearance of Black solidarity lies a matrix of attitudes about skin color and features in which color, not character, establishes friendships; degree of lightness, not expertise, influences hiring; and complexion, not talent, dictates casting for television and film.

Traditionally, the color complex involved light-skinned Blacks' rejection of Blacks who were darker. Increasingly, however, the color complex shows up in the form of dark-skinned African

Americans spurning their lighter-skinned brothers and sisters for not being dark enough. – Russell, Wilson, Hall (1992)

It appears that the pendulum has swung back in the direction of preference toward lighter-skinned Blacks, if you ask me. Either way, the color complex certainly remains an issue that plagues the Black community today. So the concern is whether this forthcoming information about melanin will fuel even more confusion with regard to the color complex.

Both of the aforementioned matters are real and have far-reaching implications: the cry of reverse racism and the concern of color preference in the Black community. To ignore their validity, or to pretend that these issues will not cause a level of discomfort for many people, is simply not realistic. Yet is it enough to keep us from acknowledging, discussing, and spreading the scientific truth about melanin?

From many will emerge the common response that we're all human and that we should not distinguish or discuss differences amongst the races. In other words, "Can't we all just get along?" T. Owens Moore, a noted scholar in the field of melanin, aptly responds in his book, *Dark Matters – Dark Secrets*: *"Of course we all just want to get along, but to negate the biogenetic factors that dictate melanin functioning disallows a true interpretation of how genes can influence behavior."*

Contemplate this: everything is made of atoms, which bond in different configurations to form molecules; the molecules manifest into different objects; yet, all of the objects originated from the same source and are part of the One.

So, too, are we humans, all from the One. Yet there are variations; there are differences; there are distinctions…and it's okay!

Lions and tigers and bears, oh my! That's life. In nature, the lions are not mad at the tigers, and the tigers are not mad at the bears. We, as humans, must step outside of the norms, or the socialized systems of beliefs that have been engineered for us and designed to control thoughts and actions to a predetermined end. We must acknowledge the commonalities and distinctions for what they are. Step outside the box; ask the questions; and search for the answers.

The Chicken Coop

Consequently, I would like to share a story with you entitled, "The Chicken Coop." One day some chicks discovered the egg of an eagle that had found its way into the chicken coop. No one knew where the egg came from. It looked a little different, yet it was an egg, and there was a baby inside that needed nurturing and care. So the hens placed the egg in the nest, sat on it, and nurtured the egg until it hatched.

When the egg hatched, out came a strange-looking baby "chick." It looked different from the other chicks, but the hens cared for it just the same. The baby eaglet grew up with the other chicks. He thought he was a chick too, so he acted like the chicks.

From time to time, the other chicks ridiculed and teased him for being different, causing him to feel less than worthy. Having no reference to know that he was an eaglet and that he *was* different, he just continued on trying to fit in and act as much like the chicks as possible.

Now, although chickens are birds, they don't fly very well and can only do so for short distances and low altitudes. In as much as the eaglet thought he was a chick, while imitating the other chicks, he never really tried to fly far or high. But all the while, emanating from deep within, there was a yearning.

One day the yearning caused him to fly just a little higher than the other chickens. The next day, he tried it again and flew even higher. Now he was beginning to realize there *was* something different about him. He didn't know what it was, but he knew it felt right; it felt good.

Omiyale Jubé

Finally, he took off, soared to great heights, and never looked back. He became aware of who he was and the great potential that he possessed within. Back in the coop, the chickens just watched as the eaglet soared away.

Now, do you think that the chickens in the chicken coop were saying, "Hey? That's reverse racism!" *Lions and tigers and bears, oh my!*

The universe is in exact order. We are all a part of the One. Each of us came here for a specific purpose. We each chose the body with which to experience this life's existence. Each of us has a part to play in the grand universal scheme.

The Disconnect

Now that we have explored and discovered how awesome melanin is, the question becomes: If melanin is so powerful, why are so many people lost and detached? There has got to be a disconnect somewhere.

I have seen individuals with less melanin than I who seemed to be so connected to the Life Force energy. And then I have seen others with lots of melanin who seem extremely disconnected and lost. Why is that?

A proper response to these questions would require considerable discussion in which I, not being a scientist, am not prepared to lead; thus, I relinquish the responsibility of a thorough explanation to the scientists and scholars. However, I would like to address two areas of significant relevance.

The first issue has to do with the amount of exposure to the sun, since it is the sunlight that causes melanin to be produced in many areas of the body and provide a life-sustaining source for our mind, body, and soul. Yet, lack of knowledge and the negative stigma associated with the color black and dark skin cause some persons of color to shy away from spending too much time in the sun, afraid that their complexion will become "too dark."

In many cases it is the same stigma that causes people to use bleaching agents to lighten the skin or hair dye to lighten and destroy the natural melanin in the hair. It is my hope that the results of the research on melanin and its awesome capabilities will soon become known in the mainstream and encourage individuals to increase their exposure to the sun. (See the section in this chapter about sunlight.)

A second reason for the apparent disconnect from the awesome capabilities of melanin is due to the level of toxicity in our bodies.

Whether external or internal, the occurrence of melanin is to protect tissue from the damaging effects of toxic substances. (Moore 2002)

Melanin not only protects us from the harmful ultraviolet rays of the sun, but it also serves to protect our bodies from all sorts of toxins we inhale or ingest.

Melanin will bind to the toxic substance, hold onto it, and release the toxin in smaller and less dangerous quantities over a period of time. It is through this process that melanin protects us from unnatural and toxic substances introduced to the body. However, these same toxic substances serve to weaken the capacity for melanin to function at its highest potential.

Mother Earth is 4.5 billion years old. Unfortunately, the current levels of toxins in our environment (our air, water, and foods) are at their highest since the beginning of time. To that extent, it becomes difficult to avoid the daily inhalation and ingestion of numerous toxins. However, we need to look at some of the unnatural and dangerous substances that we willingly inhale and ingest far too often.

Toxic "Food" Substances

White Flour, White Sugar, White Rice, and Table Salt

I use the term *food* with reserve because food is that which serves to provide nutrients and nourish the body. Yet the aforementioned "foods" have been refined, processed, bleached, or otherwise stripped of their nutritional value.

Let's look at white bleached flour we use for cooking. Some of you may be old enough to remember what we used to do when we ran out of glue for our school projects. We would mix some white flour with water into a thick paste, which worked just fine as a glue replacement.

Well, that's what we are ingesting every time we eat products made from white flour: pasta, pancakes, bread, biscuits, and so forth. They become a paste that clog our arteries.

With regard to refined white sugar, it is so depleted of nutritional value that it can no longer be classified as a food.

White refined sugar is not a food. It is a chemical. It is an addictive drug. Yes, that's right, an addictive drug, and when you remove it from your diet you can experience withdrawal symptoms as excruciating and serious as alcohol withdrawal, including tremors, flu-like symptoms, headaches, and mood swings so intense you would near kill for a chocolate bar. Some say it is as addictive as heroin.

The biochemical make up of white sugar is almost identical to alcohol, except for one molecule. Refined white sugar is stripped of any nutritional value and is an empty calorie food. In addition to that, in order to be metabolized in the body it has to draw from your vitamin and mineral reserves and therefore is responsible for depleting mineral and vitamin levels, which in itself creates numerous health problems.

"Sweet Poison," *The Environmental Illness Resource*, Perkins, Cynthia, M.Ed., © 2002

Many of the popular drinks consumed mainly by our youth contain between twenty-four and thirty-five grams of sugar. Read the labels.

Legal and Illegal Drugs

Let's take a closer look at the legal drugs that Americans ingest in tremendous amounts on a daily basis—the pharmaceuticals.

The number of pharmaceuticals that are consumed in the United States on a daily basis is staggering. Americans consume more drugs than any other country, yet we as a nation have the highest recorded numbers of illness. So we consume (ingest) legal pharmaceuticals (drugs made largely from chemicals) to cure our illnesses, but are bodies are still sick (in a "dis-eased" state).

Take all of those pretty-colored capsules and pills, open them up or crush them, and what we have is a white powder that resembles the highly addictive illegal drugs. Just because they are legal does not mean they are any safer or any less toxic to your body. For many pharmaceuticals, the list of side effects is more extensive than the list of benefits they claim to provide.

With regard to illegal drugs, the other white substances, it's time that we rethink what we call our "recreational" drug usage. Inner-city neighborhoods are flooded with these substances, and we are socialized through media that illegal drugs are socially acceptable, i.e., movies, television, music, etc.

Cocaine and heroin are commonly known to be highly addictive and dangerous to our health. What we didn't know was the relationship between cocaine and melanin. Cocaine is attracted to melanin; the combination causes the drug to be even more addicting and dangerous to melanin-dominant persons. There have been numerous studies conducted on the effects of cocaine and the detrimental effects upon melanin-dominant populations.

Cocaine is a toxic drug and is attracted to melanin. When the two mix, a new chemical hybrid can be created that can cause harmful brain effects. The function of melanin is degraded and destroyed when highly reactive free radicals are formed in the brain from toxic drugs. (Moore 2002)

Illegal drug use has become part of American culture, and is overrepresented in the Black community. As we come into the knowledge of the detriment of these substances to our melanin and its capabilities, it's time to reverse this drug culture once and for all.

Well now, that's a tall order…and where do we start? I say with "one individual at a time," each person taking responsibility for his or her own existence. It begins with changing habits. Some will be able to do this on their own. Maybe begin an exercise program, join a gym, join an organization, change your habits…your normal routine. You very well may need to change your associates. Some will need assistance, which might require attending a rehabilitation facility. You know who you are.

The choice is yours; do you want to reactivate the awesome powers you possess within? Or would you prefer to continue your journey as is? Remember, only you are responsible for what shows up in your life. However, know that you are not alone. I know you are loved, so be sure to solicit the support from positive family, friends, and community organizations.

Withdrawal from the legal drugs, the pharmaceuticals, is yet another matter of major concern. Yes, I said withdrawal, because America is hooked on legal drugs. In order to reverse this alarming statistic, it is again a matter of changing our habits. One key is to enhance our health by consuming (ingesting) only that which is healthy for us and decrease the "need" for the prescription drugs that are in many cases only contributing to the "dis-eased" state of our bodies. This is an issue for me personally, since I am still held hostage by certain prescription drugs. It is a process, but as long as we are aware and headed in the right direction, the journey continues.

As we begin to provide essential fuels for our ship, our vessel moves closer to optimal performance. Upon realization of the phenomenal attributes and benefits of melanin, when we examine what we introduce into our bodies, it's no wonder we are experiencing a disconnection from our God Source Energy. What is it that we need to do to correct this imbalance of nature? We need to get our ship in order.

Reactivate Your Melanin

Never in a million years would you even consider beginning the journey of a lifetime in a ship that wasn't properly prepared for the voyage. You wouldn't set sail in a ship that wasn't clean, nor would you fill your ship with the wrong kind of fuel. That would have the makings of an uncomfortable and troublesome trek. So as we prepare our vessel, it's time to swab the decks and clean the ship from the inside out. We must also provide our ship with sufficient fuel for the trip and only fuel that qualifies as high-grade premium.

So let's begin to prepare our bodies from the inside out, from a cellular level. We've learned a considerable amount about melanin and its awesome powers. Now we need to focus on reactivating our melanin. What is it we need to do to stimulate our melanin to function once more at its greatest potential?

Free, Clean, and Renewable Energy

First and foremost, we must spend time in the sun. The sun is a major contributing factor in the production of melanin. It is the sun that promotes the melanocyte (cell) to produce melanin. We already know that melanin is a conductor of the sun's energy.

So start by spending more time outside and getting some sunlight. It's free! It is said that just fifteen minutes in the sun will produce natural vitamin D. If someone told you there was a source providing free electricity to power your home or car, I bet the lines would be down the block and around the corner.

Well, folks this is the same concept. There is FREE energy to recharge your body so your ship can function. Think about it: free, clean, renewable energy!!

Please note that persons with less melanin must use precautions while in direct sunlight to protect themselves from the ultraviolet rays of the sun. In addition, all persons should use discernment with regard to exposure to the sun; too much of anything is not wise.

Melanin Responds to What You Eat, Drink, and Think!

Next, since we now know that melanin does not like unnatural substances, we need to stop willingly ingesting processed foods and other toxins that we know to be detrimental to our melanin. Instead, we need to provide our bodies with the required fuel.

Our vessel is going to perform commensurate with what type of fuel we feed it. If we fill it with regular grade fuel, it will perform sufficiently. Accordingly, if we fill it with watered-down, low-grade fuel, it will still run. But, eventually, it's going to experience problems and break down.

If you want your ship to perform to its optimum capacity, then you must provide the best of all fuels—that which is essential. Melanin responds to what you eat, drink, and think! As we focus on identifying the fuel that is essential to reactivate our melanin, the depth of this profound statement will become more apparent.

You Are What You Eat

Melanin responds to what you eat. You've heard the expression, "You are what you eat." Let's elaborate on that concept. You are what you *ingest* into your system, by way of what you **inhale, absorb**, or **swallow**.

If we take a moment and pay attention, we would be surprised at the number of substances we **inhale** on any given day. We know that these days even the air we breathe is full of contaminants. However, there's not a lot we can do about the air other than to detoxify our bodies periodically.

To that point, let's move on and examine what we **absorb**. All substances we apply to our skin, which is our largest organ, are directly absorbed into our system. We are constantly applying all sorts of lotions, deodorants, perfumes, colognes, hair products, cosmetics, and so on. Many of the formulated products we spread upon our skin consist of unnatural, toxic substances that are poisonous to our bodies. Some of the ingredients are substances we would never dream of putting in our food or swallowing.

Once this information was brought to my attention, I decided to look at the ingredients in my cosmetics, specifically the foundation that I apply to my face. I was shocked at the list of poisons I was unwittingly smearing on my face every day! To that end, it is important to replace these unnatural products with natural substances.

A rule of thumb to keep in mind is this: if you wouldn't eat it, then don't put it on your skin. Actually, I was under the impression that my line of cosmetics was one of the more natural brands. It just goes to show the importance of reading the labels consistently.

In addition, it is equally important to examine closely what we take into our mouths and **swallow**. Our bodies are so amazing, yet they need the proper (essential) fuel to function at full capacity. Just imagine pouring glue (a mixture of flour and water) into a ship's engine. That would result in a total disaster. So too is it a disaster for your body. We have got to adjust our diets! As noted earlier, we need to replace the white sugar, white flour, white rice, and table salt with whole foods and natural, sun-enriched, colorful fruits and vegetables provided by Mother Nature.

I will not go into more detail here because we already know the routine. We've heard it so many times before: *Eat your fruits and vegetables*. When we ingest sun-enriched foods, we're actually *eating* the sun's energy! How cool is that?

Eating fresh, natural produce really will nourish your body, increase your health, and serve to reactivate your melanin. So just do it; replace the daily visit to the fast-food drive-in with a daily visit to the local vegetable stand.

Of course, changing our habits is easier said than done. Trust me; I know. I, too find myself on the roller-coaster ride, between eating correctly and sliding back into old habits. Allow me to share a couple of tricks that really helped steady my progress.

First, clear out all the unnatural, devitalized food from the cupboards and refrigerator. This forces you (encourages you) to buy healthier items and learn to cook different dishes. If you are brave, clear out everything all at once. If not feeling so rambunctious, start with a few items at a time. Decide to refrain from certain items, such as white sugar or white flour. Make the commitment to begin using brown sugar and wheat, rice, or almond flour.

Secondly, start reading the food labels. The ingredients are listed in order of percentage contained in the product. In other words, the first ingredient is the most prevalent in the food. If you are purchasing a bottle of green tea, for example, and the ingredients include ten items, you need to ask yourself what you are consuming other than tea. You will be amazed at the sheer number of ingredients listed on some of our food selections. Reading labels played a major part in my transition to healthier food choices.

Water, Water Everywhere

Melanin responds to what you drink. Water is everywhere, yet many of us dismiss its importance in our lives. We require water in order to function properly. It's just that plain and simple. The Earth is 75 percent water and so are our bodies. Also, our brain contains 80 percent water. Think about a grape, full of juice. Now think of that grape all dehydrated and you have a raisin. Our bodies will suffer a similar fate of dehydration without daily, sufficient water.

We require at least eight glasses of water per day, or sixty-four ounces. Water helps to cleanse our cells. It will actively help us lose weight as it cleanses the waste and assists in the detoxification process. It also gives a sensation of feeling full, which results in the reduction of our appetite.

Water enhances our memory. We must increase our intake of *pure* water, not tea, coffee or Kool-Aid. Pure water is one of the essential fuels that our body requires.

Now, with that said, I would be remiss if I did not take a moment to discuss the phenomenal research of the Japanese scientist, Masaru Emoto. In his book, *The Hidden Messages in Water,* Emoto shares the wondrous characteristics of water resulting from his amazing research.

In one of his most widely discussed experiments, Emoto took water from the same source and separated it into two containers. Positive words were placed on one container, and negative words were placed on the other. After a period of time, he used a high-powered microscope to view the water crystals.

Emoto discovered the crystals from the container with the positive words was clear, bright, and formed with geometrical shapes, whereas the crystals from the other container were dull and disfigured. He concluded that words have an effect on the water.

I was so fascinated by his study that I wanted to impress upon my grandchildren the relevance of the experiment—that the words we speak and hear in our conversations and music, as well as the thoughts we think, affect the very water in our bodies. So we conducted our own experiment.

We took water from a purified water source and divided it into two jars. We wrote positive words on one jar: love, joy happiness, good, God, thank you, etc. We wrote negative or low-vibrational words on the other: hate, ugly, mean, sick, etc. We let the jars sit for twenty-four hours.

Subsequently, I poured a little water from each jar into paper cups. Then I initiated a "taste test" to determine if there was any difference between the samples. Almost everyone was able to detect a difference, stating that the water from the "positive" jar tasted better. The comments included that the quality of the water from the "positive" jar was clearer, lighter, and better. My grandchildren were truly amazed to realize how their entire body was being influenced via the water within and the words in their realm.

This is just a sample of the tremendous information Emoto's research has brought forth for humanity to utilize as we discover our potential to heal our bodies and Mother Earth. I encourage you to investigate his research further. Water responding to our thoughts is the perfect seque to the concept that melanin responds to what we think.

WATER CRYSTALS

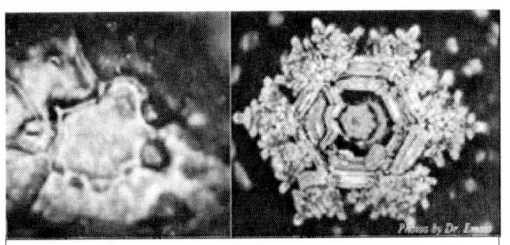

The photo on the left is of an ice crystal frozen from severely polluted water. The photo on the right is the same water refrozen after having been blessed by Dr. Emoto. One can plainly see that we do have the ability to not only heal ourselves, but our Earth as well.

Melanin and Thought

Melanin responds to what you think! The concept that melanin responds to what we think is quite profound. In other words, grab hold onto the rafters because—this gets deep!

We just touched on how thoughts affect the water in our bodies, but now we're going to examine how thoughts relate to our melanin. Okay, in order for us to comprehend this, we have to do a little bit of review.

As previously noted, we are aware that melanin is a conductor of energy. Melanin collects energy not only from the sun, but also from our environment and converts it for use in our bodies. Now, let's take a minute and review what we have learned about energy and the Universal Laws.

Energy is all there is and it is in everything. Energy, or Divine Consciousness, is aware and forms the universal mind. Energy travels in circular patterns and with purpose. From an impulse or thought, energy moves or vibrates outward with purpose, attracting like molecules, resulting in an effect or the manifestation of a physical or solid object that we perceive to be real.

Universal Law of Divine Oneness: There is but One; everything is connected; the Oneness is conscious; it is aware.

Law of Vibration: Everything vibrates and has its own frequency.

Law of Cause and Effect: Every action has an equal positive or negative reaction.

Law of Attraction: Thought and action result in the manifestation of the situation or physical object. What you think about, you bring about.

Now take a deep breath and let's look at this a little more closely.

In the beginning was the word…thought…energy. Melanin is a conductor of energy; energy is the ALL and is aware. Melanin connects our internal energy with the external energy, or in other words, melanin connects us to the One…Source Energy…or that which some may call God! Think about it. Now that's deep!

Are you getting this? Are you in awe of the magnificent vessel in your possession? I know I am!

Are you now ready to get your ship in order? Swab the deck, clean the vessel, and provide the essential fuels…proper nutrition, plenty of water, and positive "food for thought?" I get excited when I realize the capabilities…the possibilities! The power we have within! This is simply great stuff!

But wait, there is more. We've inspected, cleaned, and fueled our vessel. Now we need to locate, activate, and rev up the other engines. Yes, engines. Our vessel is hypo-charged; we have multiple engines. Stay tuned for the next chapter.

CATCH THE WAVE – *Chapter Summary*

IMPORTANT POINTS TO REMEMBER

- Melanin is the chemical key to life.
- The properties, functions, and benefits of melanin are varied and numerous.
- Melanin is a conductor of ALL types of energy: sunlight, electromagnetic, sound (music), phone waves, radio waves, heat waves, microwaves, computer radiation, radar, X-rays, cosmic rays, and ultraviolet rays.
- Melanin regulates ALL bodily functions.
- Everyone has melanin. Each individual's genetic make-up determines his or her ability to produce melanin, the type of melanin produced, and its capacity to interact with the environment.
- It is the melanin in natural "nappy" hair that causes it to grow up toward the sun, acting like antennae, drawing energy back down into our bodies.
- Melanin responds to what you eat, drink, and think.
- Melanin connects you to Divine Consciousness, God Source Energy.

ACTION STEPS

- **CELEBRATE YOUR MELANIN.** Learn everything you can about melanin because it is what makes you Black. It is what gives you your Soul. Following these action steps will help you nourish and reactivate your melanin, reconnecting you to your Source power.
- **Get out in the sunlight every day.** Fifteen minutes of sunlight will supply your daily requirement of vitamin D.

- Take a walk outdoors.
- Take a sunbath.
- Enjoy a sunrise meditation.

- **Detoxify your system**. There are many ways to detox your body. There are all types of fasts, flushes, and programs. One of my favorite is Queen Afua's 21-Day Fast from *Heal Thyself*. While you are searching for the system that best suits your needs, here is a tip to get you started. Try fasting from sundown to sundown for one day a week, (6 p.m. until 6 p.m.). This is a twenty-four hour period, and you are only skipping two meals.

- **Refrain from voluntarily ingesting toxins**:
  - Stop eating the junk food (or seriously cut back).
  - Clean out your refrigerator and cabinets of all the devitalized "food."
  - Stay away from the so-called "recreational" drugs.
  - As your health increases, decrease your dependence on legal drugs (upon the advice of your doctor).

- **Modify your diet** to include lots of sun-enriched fruits and vegetables:
  - Take a trip to your local produce store. Take a moment to look closely at the array of fruits and vegetables available. Experiment with new dishes and enjoy.
  - Explore juicing and smoothies using fresh fruits and vegetables.

- **Your body needs water**:
  - Increase your daily water intake to one-half your body weight in ounces.

    (For example, a body weight of 150 pounds requires seventy-five ounces of water)

- o Drink purified water – most tap water is contaminated with toxins.
  - o Take baths at least three times a week. Add Epsom salt (or organic vinegar if you have high blood pressure), and soak for at least fifteen-to-twenty minutes. Light a candle, massage your body, and enjoy.
- **Move your body**. Get plenty of exercise. You know the routine: Take a walk; join a gym; experience yoga or an African dance class. Just get moving!
- **Celebrate your natural nappy hair**:
  - o Experiment with natural hairstyles. Visit a natural hair salon or stylist.
  - o Keep your nappy hair happy with natural moisturizers. Do an online search for suggestions. Or try one of my favorites: distilled water with rose oil. Or shea butter, coconut oil, and lavender oil.
  - o Now you no longer have to fear the water. Go swimming at the beach; jump in that pool; take that shower with your partner!
- **Take an Extra Low Frequency (ELF) vacation:**
  - o Turn off all the screens for a day (cell phone, TV, computer, video games, radio, etc.)
  - o Go outside and enjoy nature. Take this one-step further and travel outside of the city, away from all the cell towers and electrical wiring.

LIFE LESSONS FOR TRANSFORMATION

Have you ever asked yourself why is it that African Americans seem to rank consistently among the highest statistics when it comes to poor health-related issues, such as high blood pressure, stroke, diabetes, cancer, and obesity? Why is it that African Americans have a significantly higher death rate than any other group in the United States? Much of the information circulating attributes these statements largely to poor diet, lack of exercise, and economics—for example, lack of access to affordable health care. I don't doubt the validity of the aforementioned information playing an integral part in the resulting statistics.

However, after being exposed to the research on melanin, there are some questions that surface.

Is there a correlation between these devastating statistics and the lack of knowledge and attention to your high levels of melanin? Are you eating a diet that is conducive or destructive to melanin-dominant people? Are the medications that are being prescribed for you (that are based on European physiology) safe or correct for *your* different physiological make-up? Are you being given health and lifestyle advice that is conducive to *your* well-being (for example, the advice to stay out of the sun)?

These are just a few of the questions that pop into my mind. This is serious business. If you earnestly act upon the action steps listed above, I believe that the current statistics on health-related issues for African Americans could be drastically reduced, beginning with you and your family!

In addition to improving your health, could you stand to have a youthful appearance, fewer wrinkles, more energy, long life (anti-aging), improved memory, enhanced intuition, enlightenment, and heightened connection to the Divine? Talk about life-changing! Know Thyself—Knowledge IS powerful!

REACTIVATE Your Energy Sources

Chapter 8

Ignite the Internal Flames

When you think of a magnificent ship and you envision the engine, my guess is that you would imagine an engine of substantial size. Amazingly, our bodies have not just one, but seven engines. These engines are called chakras, and just like any engine, each chakra needs to be fueled, maintained, and revved up for optimal performance.

Although there are seven individual chakras, they work together in a system. The chakra system affects our mental, physical, and spiritual well-being; in other words, our mind, body, and soul. Each chakra is a center of energy that spins like a wheel, drawing in energy from its environment. The chakras are often represented by a wheel or flower. The faster the chakra spins or vibrates, the more spokes on the wheel or more petals on the flower are depicted.

As previously stated, we know that energy travels in a circular motion and vibrates. Similarly, the energy of each chakra travels in a circular motion and vibrates in a vortex. A vortex is a whirling mass of air, water, or in this case, energy. Vortices are known for drawing into their realm everything that surrounds them. Again, with regard

THE CHAKRA SYSTEM

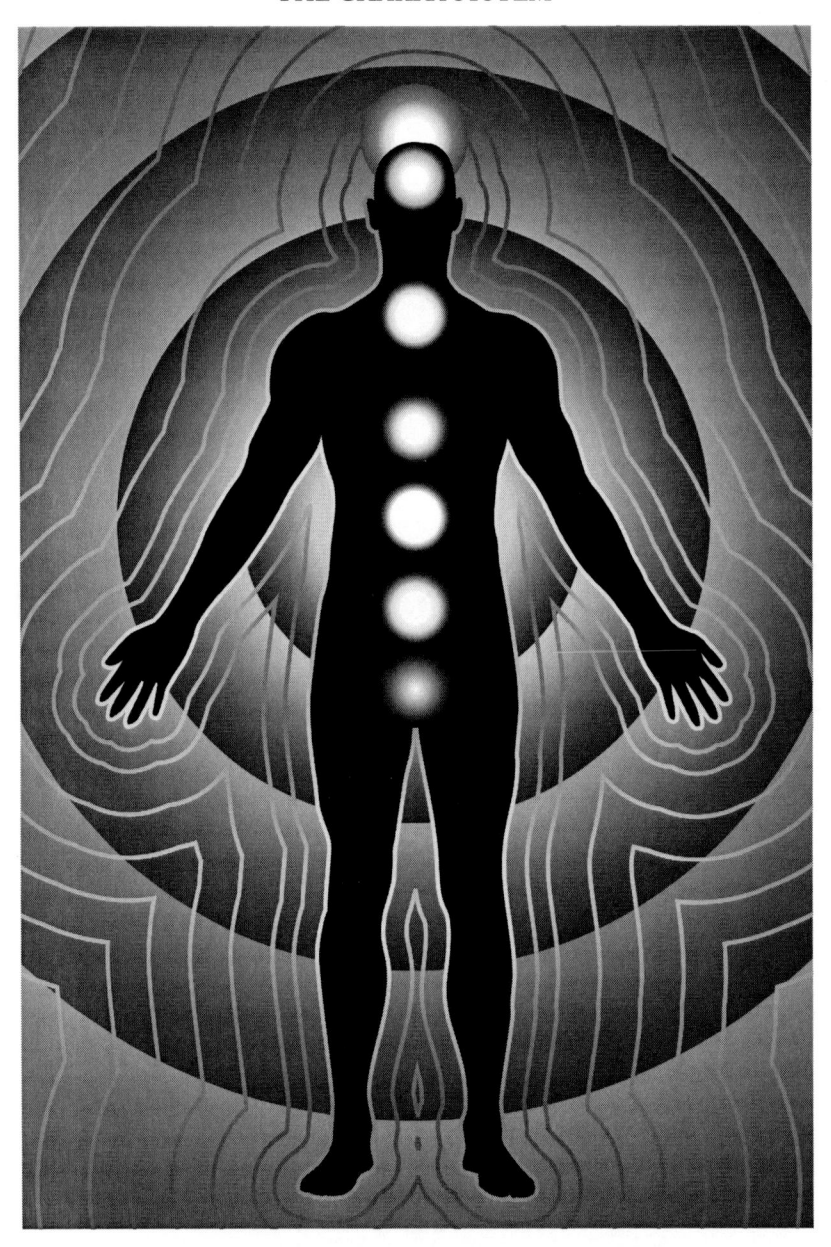

Seven Energy Centers…Seven Engines all ready to be
Revved Up for Optimal Performance

to chakras, the vortex draws in all types of energy in the surrounding environment. Every individual chakra vibrates at its own frequency, which contributes to the various characteristics exhibited by the chakra. Any given chakra is identified by number, name, location, color, emotion, and function.

For example, let's explore the Fourth Chakra.

Number:	Fourth
Name:	Heart Chakra
Location:	Center of the Chest
Color:	Light Green
Emotion(s):	Love, Compassion
Function(s):	Trust and Forgiveness

(Author's Note: See chart and locate each chakra center)

Heaven and Earth

The phenomenon of chakras is an ancient art and has been interpreted by many cultures over the years. As you continue to research the amazing world of chakras, you will find there are many other characteristics and/or functions for individual chakras. In addition, you will encounter varying information and points of view, ranging from variations in the colors to varying information on the functions.

CHAKRA CHART

Chakra	Function	Location	Emotion	Color
7th - Crown	Spiritual - Enlightenment and Vision	Crown of the Head	Bliss	Violet
6th – Third Eye	Intuition and Vision	Center Brow	Inspiration	Indigo
5th - Throat	Communication and Self-Expression	Base of the Neck Center of the Collarbone	Healing Nature	Blue
4th - Heart	Love and Compassion	Center of Chest	Trust and Forgiveness	Green
3rd - Solar Plexus	Strength and Will Power	Two inches above the Navel	Self Control	Yellow
2nd – Sacral	Creativity and Procreation	Two inches below the Navel	Desires	Orange
1st – Root	Security and Survival	Base of the Spine	Protection	Red

Isn't it amazing how it all fits together? Like a Multi-Dimensional Jigsaw Puzzle. It's all energy. You are energy. Energy is the All, and the All is aware-conscious.

The chakras represent heaven and earth within our bodies. The three lower chakras are grounding chakras representing the earth. They connect us to our earthly or physical needs, wants, and desires. The three higher chakras are the more spiritual chakras representing our more heavenly and Divine nature. The Fourth Chakra is the bridge or gateway connecting the two worlds within. It represents the center of unconditional love that is needed to enter into the higher realms.

As you explore the chakra system, the comparisons to the seven dimensions become more apparent. Within our bodies we have the representation of heaven and earth. "As Above, So Below; As Within, So Without," from *The Seven Cosmic Principles of Thoth*.

Consequently, when our chakra system is balanced and activated, we are in alignment with our earthly and heavenly environment. When mind, body, and soul are in alignment, we are just plain healthier and happier. Isn't it amazing how it all fits together? Like a Multi-Dimensional Jigsaw Puzzle. It's all energy. You are energy. Energy is the All, and the All is aware-conscious.

Each chakra needs to be balanced and energized in order for the body to function properly. Chakras can be blocked, underactive, or overactive, causing an imbalance in our overall system. If one chakra is out of balance, it can throw the neighboring chakras off and we will feel out of sync. Our chakras need oxygen, sunlight, good nutrition, water, and movement (exercise). Some of the causes of imbalance can be the lack of any one of these aspects. Also, our chakras react adversely to negative thoughts, sounds, and toxins of any kind.

Sunlight is white. If you shine the sun's rays through a prism, the light refracts into the seven colors of the rainbow, each color traveling at a different speed. Our chakras react the same way. Each chakra spins and vibrates at a different speed. The faster the vibration: the lighter the color, the higher the sound, and the higher the frequency.

One way to activate the chakras is to get lots of sunlight. Eating foods compatible with the color of the chakra also help stimulate the corresponding chakra (for example red apples, for the red root chakra). Of course we know how important water is to our energy, so drink lots of pure water for active, healthy chakras. Chakras need oxygen, which brings us to or next topic, yoga.

Yoga and the Chakra System

It never ceases to amaze me that, although I completed years of schooling from grade school through several institutions of higher learning and hold several degrees, I was never introduced to the chakra system during the course of my education.

In biology I learned all about the body and the workings of the digestive, respiratory, and circulatory systems. Yet, not a word was ever mentioned about the amazing chakra system. Why? My sister introduced me to the concept of chakras a long time ago. But it was not until I connected with the ancient art of yoga that I learned the intricate world of the chakras—how they enable us to ignite the power within and connect to the energy of the universe.

In the past, I used to think of yoga as a form of exercise that required one to contort the body into some seemingly painful positions and maintain them for hours. This certainly can be true, especially for the more advanced practitioners, so I just wasn't interested in exploring the discipline.

At some point I discovered that there are many different types of yogic practices, so I began my research. Initially, I enrolled in a yoga class that consisted of stretching and deep breathing. The class focused on deep relaxation and increasing the oxygen circulating in the body. Now this was much more appealing to me than the thought of contorting into painful yogic positions. I really enjoyed my classes and always left feeling extremely relaxed and pleasant. Yet, I still viewed yoga as more of an exercise rather than a discipline, or way of life.

At any rate, it was not until I joined a yoga practice, as opposed to just taking a basic class, that I learned a more holistic definition of yoga: a discipline for achieving union with Supreme Spirit through meditation, prescribed postures, and controlled breathing. I now possessed more of an understanding that yoga is not just about physical conditioning. All in all, it is a discipline or practice affording you the ability to align your mind, body, and spirit, enabling you to connect with the universal source of energy. As I continued to study, I increasingly expanded my comprehension of the definition of yoga.

Teacher and author Richard Hittleman offers this definition: *Yoga is essentially an experience, not a philosophy. It is to be lived, not understood. To achieve this, meditation is indispensable!*

Subsequently, it is an ancient art form with many variations.

While traveling in Kemet/Egypt, I discovered that yoga was a part of *my* ancient cultural heritage. Our ancestors practiced yoga literally thousands of years ago. Proof of this is evident through depictions of yogic postures etched into stone in the Kemetic/Egyptian temples and pyramids. In addition, there are also stone etchings of energy healing, similar to what one would call Reiki, or the laying on of hands.

Now it's time for you to bring the past traditions into the present…time to utilize the wisdom of the ancestors to reactivate the power within. Here again, it is important to employ your due diligence; research various types of yoga, such as hatha, kemetic, or kundalini. Try different types of practices and you will find one that resonates with your mind, body, and soul.

Activating the Engines

Now that we've discovered that we possess seven engines, or seven energy centers called chakras, it is time to learn an excellent means of activation. How do we energize them, rev them up, and prepare to set sail?

Chakras are awakened and activated by drawing in energy. We know that energy is aware, so the process of activation all begins with thought. The idea is to bring your attention and breath to the chakra you want to energize for optimal results. The procedure begins with the mind—thought and attention.

Where the mind goes, energy follows.

Where energy goes, so does the breath.

Where the breath goes, so does oxygen, activating the area.

Yes, it takes practice, but it's so simple and it's free!

Of course, this is activation at a very primary level. The more disciplined you become in the practice, the deeper the levels of concentration.

Just imagine being able to activate or start the engine of your car or ship simply with concentration and breathing. Well, that's all it takes for the initial stages of activation. What's more, you have seven engines at your service to propel you forth into higher realms of existence.

With just simple breathing exercises, you can begin the process of activating your chakras. Of course the more you focus your attention and the more advanced your breathing techniques become, the higher the levels of activation can be achieved.

With that said, let's get going and put this information into practice. My suggestion for this next section is that you read it first for understanding. Next, review it while practicing the steps. Finally, when you feel comfortable with the process, attempt the procedure with your eyes closed. The more you practice, the more confident you will feel and the system will become second nature.

Get Ready, Get Set – Breathe!

Preparation

Find a quiet place and time where you will not be disturbed. Be sure to wear comfortable clothing—something loose and unrestrictive—so you can breathe freely. Select a straight-back chair.

Before we begin, let's take a moment to locate each chakra by gently touching the area.

7th Chakra/ Crown	Located in the center/top of your head
6th Chakra/Third Eye	Located right between your eyebrows
5th Chakra/Throat	Located at the base of your neck, center of your collar bone
4th Chakra/Heart	Located in the center of your chest
3rd Chakra/Solar Plexus	Located two inches above the navel
2nd Chakra/Sacral	Located two inches below the navel
1st Chakra/Root	Located right between the genitals and the anus
	(Just squeeze and envision the area)

To release the tension of the day, gently shake your body, your arms, your legs, etc. That should feel better already. Sit in the chair with your spine straight and slightly away from the back of the chair. Imagine a string coming out of the top of your head; now pull it up and straighten your body. Sit with your feet flat on the floor, preferably barefoot. Place your hands on your thighs close to your knees, palms facing up or down, whichever is more comfortable to you. There, now you are in position.

Cleansing Breaths

Take a deep breath in through your nose, open your mouth wide, and really blow the breath out through your mouth. This is called a Cleansing Breath. Repeat the cleansing breath two more times. It helps to clear your breathing passageways. Sometimes it may cause you to cough. That's just fine; it lets you know the process is working to clear your breathing channels. And if at any time should you feel lightheaded or uncomfortable in any way, simply stop. When you're ready, you can always begin again.

Relaxing Breaths

Next we're going to take three relaxing breaths to still our bodies and minds. First, let's review and practice the process. Inhale through the nose to the count of four. As you inhale through the nose, mentally follow your breath up to the top of your head. Hold the breath to the count of four. Now exhale slowly through your mouth to the count of four. As you exhale, drop and relax your jaw, following the breath from the top of your head straight down to the base of your spine.

Ready? Let's begin with three relaxing breaths:

Slowly inhale through the nose to the count of four, following the breath up to the top of your head.
Hold…2, 3, 4.
Exhale through the mouth, following the breath straight down to the base of your spine…2, 3, 4.
Relax.
Repeat the relaxing breath two more times.
Great job!

Igniting the Flame

Next, we're going to repeat this process—only this time we're going to concentrate on each chakra, one at a time.

So let's begin with your attention on the Crown Chakra.

Slowly inhale through the nose to the count of four, following the breath up above your head,
Hold…2, 3, 4.
Exhale, through your mouth, while concentrating on your Seventh or Crown Chakra…2, 3, 4.
Relax.
Slowly inhale through the nose to the count of four, following the breath up above your head.
Hold…2, 3, 4.
Exhale through your mouth, while concentrating on your Sixth chakra, your Third Eye…2, 3, 4.
Relax.
Slowly inhale through the nose to the count of four, following the breath up above your head.
Hold…2, 3, 4.
Exhale through your mouth, while concentrating on your Fifth or Throat Chakra…2, 3, 4.
Relax.
Slowly inhale through the nose to the count of four, following the breath up above your head.
Hold…2, 3, 4.
Exhale through your mouth, while concentrating on your Fourth or Heart Chakra…2, 3, 4 .
Relax.

Slowly inhale through the nose to the count of four, following the breath up above your head.

Hold…2, 3, 4.

Exhale through your mouth, while concentrating on your Third or Solar Plexus Chakra…2, 3, 4.

Relax.

Slowly inhale through the nose to the count of four, following the breath up above your head.

Hold…2, 3, 4.

Exhale through your mouth, while concentrating on your Second or Sacral Chakra…2, 3, 4.

Relax.

Slowly inhale through the nose to the count of four, following the breath up above your head.

Hold…2, 3, 4.

Exhale through your mouth, while concentrating on your First or Root Chakra…2, 3, 4.

Relax.

And now, as you come back into the present moment, inhale deeply and exhale through the mouth, really blowing the breath out.

Again, inhale deeply, and exhale through the mouth.

Once again, inhale deeply, and exhale through the mouth.

Wiggle your feet and wiggle your hands. When you're ready, open your eyes….

Congratulations! You have just begun the process to awaken and energize your chakras. You are well on the way to rev up your seven engines in preparation for extended travel.

Of course this is a process and it takes practice. If you are new to this technique, you have just placed the key in the ignition. In order to really rev up the engines and activate them to full capacity, it takes focus, discipline, and commitment. As you continue to study, you will uncover many techniques to energize your chakras and fine-tune them to optimal condition. The more the chakras are activated the more expansive the territories available for your exploration.

All in all, the chakra system is intricate, and this is merely an introduction. As you continue on your journey of exploration, each of you will travel as fast or as slowly as is comfortable for you. We each have our own routes to take to arrive at our desired destinations. As you learn to energize your chakras, you will learn how to find that inner peace and balance so many are searching for.

Inspection of the Vessel

The Light Body

In the examination of your remarkable vessel, I would be remiss if I didn't at least touch on a topic that plays a monumental part in the constitution of the Total You: *The Light Body*.

Each person has an energy source or light body within that brings together our physical, mental, emotional, and spiritual being. This light is our Life Force, accessed only by going within. Actually, it is an extension of the light energy of your chakras.

When we discuss the concept that all human beings are connected to the ultimate source, it is this energy—this light body within—that connects everyone all the way back, through each of the dimensions, to the original source…the All, the One, Infinite Source—God. Think of your energy as having "no beginning and no end."

So, in actuality, a part of you (your energy and your light) exists in each of the dimensions simultaneously. As the energy that is you descends from the higher dimensions to the Third Dimension, a bit of your essence remains in each dimension. Remember, there is only the One and all of our energy is connected. Okay, I know I may have gone too far out there for some readers, so I won't attempt to delve into this topic too deeply. What is important to understand is that we are all ultimately from the same Source.

The Physical Body

Our bodies are truly amazing. Anyone who has ever studied biology cannot help but be amazed at the masterpiece that is the human body. Before we leave this section, how about some interesting facts about *the physical body*?

- The brain operates very much like a computer, with all of its high-tech functionality. The computer was actually designed and based on the human brain. Nerve impulses to the brain travel up to 170 miles per hour.
- The human heart beats 80,000 times a day, which adds up to 40,000,000 times a year. We have 60,000 miles of blood vessels in our body; that is enough to circle the Earth 2.5 times.
- If our entire DNA was stretched out end to end, it could reach the moon and back 3,000 times.
- Three hundred million cells die in the human body every minute. With the exception of the first eight cells formed after conception, all other cells in the human body are completely regenerated approximately every seven years. Some are saying that now the process of regeneration only takes two years. If true, that would further validate that things are truly speeding up.
- A brain cell looks amazingly similar to the shape of the universe. "As Above, So Below; As Within, So Without"
- Pound per pound, the human body produces more energy than the sun!

Unbelievable!!!

Yes, we already are titleholders to the most amazing vessel on the planet. It's ours and we own it "free and clear." We are free to do with it what we "will."

Our vessel truly is amazing, from our light body which is an extension of our chakras or seven energy centers, on to the physical structure. It is astonishing to think of the awesome powers we possess within and never knew!

A BRAIN CELL - THE UNIVERSE

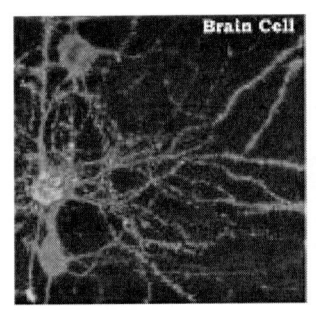

Mark Miller
Source: Mark Miller;
Brandeis University;
Virgo Consortium
for Cosmological
Supercomputer Simulations;
www.visualcomplexity.com

Virgo Consortium
The New York Times

CATCH THE WAVE – *Chapter Summary*

IMPORTANT POINTS TO REMEMBER

- The chakra system consists of seven energy centers that contribute to the well-being of our mental, physical, and spiritual bodies.
- When the chakras are balanced and in alignment with our earthly and heavenly environment, we are naturally healthier and happier.
- Chakras may be blocked, underactive, or overactive, causing an imbalance in our overall system.
- Each chakra has various characteristics and functions.
- Chakras need oxygen, sunlight, good nutrition, water, and movement.
- Chakras respond negatively to low-vibrational thoughts, sounds, and all toxins.
- We possess a light body which is an extension of our chakra system.
- A part of you exists on all seven dimensions simultaneously.
- This is your journey to reconnect to your higher selves and/or to the Divine.
- The vessel we call the Human Body is simply amazing.

ACTION STEPS

- Continue your education on the chakra system. A wealth of information is available and we have only scratched the surface.
- Earnestly practice activating your chakras.
- Get plenty of natural light. Sunlight is a natural stimulant to the chakras.
- Join a yoga practice. Research and experiment with various

styles until you find one that suits you. Then begin to practice at your comfort level.
- Check to see if your chakras are balanced. Seek out a Reiki Master; these practitioners can "see" your energy field and let you know which chakras need adjusting and do so accordingly.
- Get plenty of fresh air. Open the windows—spend time outdoors.
- Eat live, sun-enriched, colorful foods—plenty of fruits and vegetables.
- Laugh aloud often—just because. It will raise your vibration.

LIFE LESSONS FOR TRANSFORMATION

Activating your chakras and keeping them balanced and in alignment offers you so many benefits, many of which you were most likely unaware. Many people are just coming into the knowledge that chakras exist, as well as their characteristics and functions. Keeping your chakras in alignment will keep your mind, body, and spirit in tune:

Mentally: –Providing calm, better focus, and mental clarity

Physically: –Less Stress – Reducing strain on the body, lowering blood pressure and reducing heart problems, such as stroke and/or heart attack
–Experience healthier glands and body parts that correspond to particular chakras.

Spiritually: –Connection to Higher Self/Source Energy/God
–Increased intuition – enjoy having more experiences of "knowing" the answers
–Increased Inspiration (Increased "In-Spiritness")

In addition, keeping your chakras in alignment will keep you in tune with others so you can enjoy healthier relationships. Your calm, balance, and harmony can change your reaction to situations. Maybe for you this means no more road rage. This can really be helpful, especially when you notice your four-year-old is repeating your choice words for that guy who just cut you off. Aha! Perhaps it means that, instead of snapping at your spouse, you maintain your composure and choose to share your thoughts at a later date, in a more calm and productive manner.

Your calm is contagious. This might show up as people around you begin to respond with a new level of calm. Imagine having a better relationship with your teenager. Wouldn't it be great if your boss was not as aggravating as he or she used to be? Or maybe you are dealing with him/her on a whole new level and the situation doesn't bother you like it used to. Oh, the possibilities…

Furthermore, keeping your chakras in alignment synchronizes you with the pulse of the Earth.

Yes, the Earth does have a pulse, or a heartbeat, if you will. And, when your chakras are in alignment, you vibrate at a rate comparable to the pulse of the Earth, resulting in a harmonic resonance.

In other words, when you and your chakras are in alignment, your body functions better and you just feel better. No more feeling out of whack or off-kilter—or at least now you have the tools to regain balance and harmony. Being in alignment means you are in *atonement* with the planet and the universe. *Atone-ment*: Your mind, body, and soul are in tune. *At-one-ment*: You are at one…one with the All—the Source.

Wow! Who knew all the benefits of cultivating your chakra system? In fact, we have really just scratched the surface. With regard to the chakra system, the more extensive your research and disciplined your practice, the more profound the benefits. And to think, just a decade ago Western society barely discussed the chakra system.

Yes, it is time to get back to the wisdom of our ancestors—quickly!

And we are well on our way…but first, we have one more port of call.

PART THREE

All Systems Go!
Getting Underway

The Scarab Beetle
Kemetic/Egyptian Symbol of Resurrection

All Systems Go!

Getting Underway

Introduction

WELL, MY NAUTICAL MATES, IT'S BEEN QUITE AN ESCAPADE thus far. All that's left to do now is to connect the revved-up engines to the propellers directing our destination and All Systems Go! You will have everything you need to discover your internal compass, chart your course, and travel to untold destinations. But first, let's take a moment to recap some of the routes traveled thus far.

Not an ordinary venture, this journey is an expedition of a lifetime, thus requiring extraordinary commitment and dedication. That being said, so far we've covered quite a bit of ground. Recognizing the anchors of limitation sets the course in motion. The acquisition and digestion of a multitude of knowledge, skills, and techniques required considerable amounts of time and patience. And the preparation of our vessel also required attention to detail.

Expanding our horizons and stepping out of our comfort zone allowed us to explore energy on many different levels and from various perspectives. It's amazing to see how it all fits together, sort of like pieces in a multidimensional jigsaw puzzle. The profound realization that energy is in everything afforded an opening to the concepts that Energy is the All, the One, and energy is aware…it is conscious.

Whether or not we accept it, our lives are affected by forces in both the physical (seen) world and the metaphysical (unseen) world. Understanding the seven dimensions allows us to determine our direction and our destination. Our direction is upward, or ascension; our destination is to return to consciousness, Universal Mind, or awareness of the One. A universal GPS is available for us to plot out our course, and the Universal Laws provide the guidelines upon which to frame our behaviors and actions.

How we utilize the laws, or act upon them, determines our direction. Either we will ascend into the higher realms of existence on the more spiritual planes (the heavenly realms or the metaphysical world), or we will descend and remain on the lower realms of existence (the earthly realms or the physical world).

Remember that we have Free Will. It's all up to *you* to decide!

The magic of melanin teaches us the importance of cleaning our ship from the inside out—the importance of detoxing our system. We acquired information on the essential fuels our vessel requires for optimum performance. We must nourish our bodies with the proper food, drink, and positive thoughts. The realization that melanin is a conductor of energy and that energy is Life Force—the conscious All—is purely astounding!

Seven engines—Wow! We have identified our seven chakras, or energy centers, located within our bodies. We now know how to activate them, or power them up for travel to untold destinations.

The only procedure left in the sequence is to connect our revved-up engines to the propellers and thrust our vessels forth to destinations near and far! It is time to "Set Sail" or, in nautical terms, "Get Underway!" This brings us to Prayer and Meditation in conjunction with the Law of Attraction.

RECLAIM Your Power

Chapter 9

Sailing the High Seas

Prayer and Meditation

BROUGHT UP IN THE BAPTIST CHURCH, I WAS SOMEWHAT familiar with the concept of prayer, though I later found out that I was not trained *how* to pray. In contrast, with respect to meditation, I had no frame of reference to conceptualize the notion; no idea what it meant or how to practice it. Furthermore, I certainly had no clue that prayer and meditation worked in unison to manifest our dreams and desires.

Prayer and meditation constitute the last piece of the multidimensional jigsaw puzzle that pulls it all together. Through prayer and meditation, supported by all the knowledge and techniques we've accumulated throughout our voyage, our desires become realities. Prayer and meditation (along with the Law of Attraction, which we address here) are what sets our ship into forward motion, thrusting us out on the open seas sailing toward our desired destinations. Since they are such an integral part of our voyage, it behooves us to take some time and really ascertain the profound significance of prayer and meditation. Acquiring a more holistic understanding of these methodologies will enable us to better utilize the techniques to optimize our journey.

Let's begin by taking a look at the more commonly understood definitions of prayer and meditation.

> Pray: to ask; request in a humble manner; to offer devout petition to God
> Prayer: the act or practice of praying to God
> Meditate: to focus thoughts; to reflect; to ponder; to plan or project in the mind
> Meditation: the act or practice of meditating

Upon examination of the terms, I would assume we all agree on the very basic definition of prayer as talking to God. As we continue on, we will engage further in more penetrating interpretations of prayer. With regard to the terms *meditate/meditation*, the aforementioned definitions are more academic in nature. Our purposes here demand more of a metaphysical definition of the terms.

From a metaphysical prospective, *meditation* means: a practice of entering the mind in a deep state of relaxation. It generally entails clearing the mind of all chatter and thought, or focusing on a single word, thought, or intent. It is my hope that this connotation of meditation affords a broader base of understanding for our discussion. All of these definitions are subjective and open to interpretation. My intention is to provide some common ground as we proceed in efforts to expand our perspectives.

Someone once said to me that prayer is talking to God, and meditation is listening to God. During prayer you *ask* God for what you want, need, and desire. And, in meditation, you still your mind and body so you can *listen* to God, and receive the answers.

That being said, please allow me to share my evolution with the terms *prayer* and *meditation*, from my early understandings (or lack thereof) to my current level of awareness. The more conscious/aware I became of the vast information that continues to unfold before me, the deeper my understanding of the terms, their meaning, and how to utilize them to effect change in my life.

Prayer: Ask and Ye Shall Receive

As a child and young adult, my thoughts on prayer stemmed from my foundation in the church and were largely based on the adage: "Ask and ye shall receive." I was taught that if you pray to God for what you want, you would receive it because God answers our prayers. With respect to all the praying I was exposed to, it seemed that everyone was always begging and pleading for something, myself included. It just didn't feel right. I wondered, "Why is everyone constantly asking God for something…anything…and everything?"

In addition, it didn't seem to be working. I wasn't getting the things I was praying for, so I simply stopped. It seemed to me that if I wanted something, I needed to put forth some type of effort to get it. To make my point, it seemed that these age-old adages were in alignment with my thinking: "Seek and ye shall find," and "Knock and the door shall open." If you notice, both adages suggest that there is an action needed on our part in order to receive from God, or Source.

We create our own reality. We have the power within. This caused me to analyze these adages from a different frame of reference. I was taught to look externally for someone—"God"—to not only answer my requests, but also *save* me from "myself."

Let's look at that notion through the perspective of Universal Law, or the concept of energy, taking the process of prayer step by step.

In order to pray, we must first have a thought in mind. We must think of or decide what it is we want, need, or desire.

Thought is that first impulse in the Oneness: the Universal Law of One.

The next step in the process is that we must ask for it and speak the word into existence.

Speak the word, allowing it to vibrate out into the universe, causing an effect. This incorporates the Law of Vibration, the Law of Cause and Effect, and the Law of Attraction.

Okay, when I think of prayer in conjunction with the understanding of the Universal Laws and how they work, prayer takes on a whole new meaning. Comprehending the power of my word and understanding the process of the vibration of that thought traveling out and interacting with particles and manifesting into that which I first uttered, results in my ability to conceptualize prayer, how it works, and why.

Better yet, I now know *how* to pray. I no longer "ask" the universe or God Source Energy as if I'm begging. There is no need to beg. It's a matter of "asking" in the proper manner. I decide what I desire and set my thought into motion, consciously and with intention. I now know the power of thought and the power of the word, yet I realize that this is just part of the process. I also know that along with the word comes the responsibility of some action on my part if I want to manifest my desires into fruition.

Next, I understand the need to meditate; the importance of achieving balance and harmony with Source; the importance of connecting the inner self with my higher self; and aligning mind, body, and soul so I can "hear" the answers.

Meditation: Silence Is Golden

In my youth, I recall hearing the phrase "silence is golden" and for the life of me I could never derive any sense from it. Its meaning escaped me for years until I finally encountered meditation. As has been noted, meditation remains as one of those metaphysical concepts associated with the occult. I must admit that I was afraid to meditate for many years, thanks to the fear instilled in me from my previous teachings in the church.

My continued quest and search for answers led me to explore meditation from a different perspective. Thus, as I dared to step out of my comfort zone, I discovered meditation as a vehicle to enhance my existence. Moreover, it is a process enabling us to quiet the "thinking" mind. It provides an opportunity to still all that noise that is constantly rattling on in our heads all day long: that last song we heard when we got out of the car; the commercial we heard on the TV last night; the cell phone conversation overheard in the store; all the negative self-talk; all the chitchat that just never stops. In meditation, we still the chatter inside our head so we can go within. We quiet the mind, to achieve higher levels of consciousness allowing us to connect with God Source Energy. So—silence really is golden.

As previously mentioned, many people think that in order to meditate they must hold strange yogic positions and chant for hours. While this may be true for some, it is certainly not required to engage in meditation. As a matter of fact, this presents a perfect opportunity to touch on the connection between yoga and meditation. Although people interchange the terms *yoga* and *meditation*, the terms are not wholly synonymous.

In the previous chapter, we came to know yoga as a way of life in which one aspires union with the Supreme Being through alignment of mind, body, and spirit. This can be achieved utilizing various techniques. Some yogic practices use breathing techniques; some utilize various postures and/or stretching; and some practices use a combination of both. Certainly you see how deep breathing becomes an integral aspect of the yogic discipline.

Whereas with meditation, all that is required is the quieting of your mind. As you perfect deeper meditative states, aligning your mind, body, and spirit in union with Supreme Being, ultimately you are engaged in a yogic practice. Consequently, it is easy to see why the two terms are often used synonymously.

Actually, there are numerous types and levels of meditation and/or yogic practices to choose from. It matters not which one you chose or where you start. The important thing is that you start somewhere and incorporate this powerful aspect of transformation into your journey.

As a matter of fact, you can achieve a meditative state simply by breathing deeply and bringing your attention inward. More specifically, simply taking three relaxing breaths and utilizing the process we practiced earlier to energize your chakras actuates a meditative state. So, congratulations, you already have the knowledge to begin a meditation practice. Of course, the extent of your practice will reflect the extent of your experience.

Once again, prayer and meditation represent the final segment, the ultimate components connecting everything into synchronization and the definitive elements needed to set everything into motion. At this moment, you possess everything required to Reclaim the Power… the power that once was ours as a people. Reclaim the power that resides within!

So the question becomes "Now that I've acquired all of this information, what do I do with it?" This leads us to our next segment.

Manifest the Life You Desire and Deserve

Thus far along our adventure, we've explored the cosmos and trekked through the dimensions. We've discovered melanin, cleared our chakras, and lit the flames. Now it's time to bring it home, to bring it all down to earth…and find out where the rubber meets the road.

In practical everyday terms, as I experience life day after day, what does all of this mean to me? In other words, what's in it for me?! How do I utilize this information to get more health, more wealth, better relationships, a nicer house and a good job? Finally, how do I utilize this information for personal and spiritual transformation and greater enlightenment?

It comes right back to the Universal Laws…how they affect you and how you utilize them to create your reality, no matter what your desires. In particular, it is the combination of prayer and meditation in conjunction with the Law of Attraction that guides your vessel to manifest the reality of your dreams.

Ultimately, these concepts are not as foreign or new as you may think. Upon close examination, the adages from my childhood echo the exact same principles as of the Law of Attraction. Of course, anyone prescribing to or following the Universal Laws for direction would know to look within for the answers—understanding that there is no separation between the Almighty One and the One within and realizing that we are co-creators of this universe.

It is a matter of recognizing our abilities, utilizing the knowledge and tools acquired along this journey, and reclaiming our power. Look within…everything you need resides within you. Once you become conscious of the process it just makes sense. Once you begin to practice, the process becomes more comfortable and easier.

So let's take a look at the process of prayer and meditation in conjunction with the Law of Attraction to manifest the life you desire and deserve.

Let's outline the process so you can see how simple it really is:

Thoughts	=	Decide what you want, need, desire
+		
Emotion	=	Affirm it! Speak it into being!
+		
Action	=	What must you "do" to get it?
======		================================
Manifestation	=	Results

Now let's lay out a practical application to see how this works:
- Identify what you want (thought/think about it)
- Action: Apply attention to it
- Visualize it; cut out a picture and look at it every day
- Verbalize it: write it; talk about it; speak it into existence
- Claim it with emotion; act as if you already have it. For example, if you want a car, visualize it; then *experience* the car with all of your senses, see yourself in the driver's seat, smell the new car smell, feel the leather seats, hear the sound your horn makes, taste the flavor of excitement…act like you already have it!
- What do you physically need to do to bring this further into reality? Do you need to: change your habits, change your associates, create capital (second job, savings, investment), take a class, etc.?

Is having what you want that simple? Does it work? Yes and yes! It works if you work it. It all depends on your level of application of the laws.

Case in point: Many years ago, I experienced the effects of the Law of Attraction firsthand. This was prior to knowing anything about the law or any of the Universal Laws. I was young, newly divorced, with two babies under the age of three. During the divorce, I walked away from our four-bedroom home that we had watched being built from the ground up. At the time, I was not concerned about material assets. My only concern was creating a quality life for my two sons and me.

Consequently, I found myself starting over and I had needs. So I made a list: I needed a washer and dryer, a new car, and a house to call my own. Initially, I envisioned each item in great detail. Then I found all the items in magazines, cut out the pictures, and posted them on the refrigerator along with my list, so I could see them every day. Next, I sat down and wrote out approximately how much everything would cost and what I would have to do to come up with the money. And, finally, I gave myself a time period in which to acquire everything on my list.

Looking back at every step I took, it follows the exact process one would need to pursue in order to enact the Law of Attraction. Did it work? Yes, it worked. I obtained everything on my list and before the time allotted. Awesome!

Now, does the law work so smoothly every time and for everybody? Speaking for myself, I would have to say that it does not. To illustrate the point, currently I am experiencing another major transition period in my life and the waters have been a bit choppy. I am now retired; my sons are grown and off on their own; and, oh yeah, I'm not too long out of divorce Number Two. So, yes, there are many changes in my life and *I have a list.*

Interestingly enough, this time I am not having as much success acquiring the items on my list and in the time period allotted. I've had some successes but still have a list. Now what could that mean? Does it imply that the law doesn't work?

Please remember that the laws are exact; they work *every* day and *every* time. So if you're not achieving your desired outcomes, then it's time to do some soul-searching, or some adjusting. It required that I look deeply within and figure out exactly what part of the process I was not applying correctly. Regrettably, it took me a while to figure out I was allowing *Anchors of limitation* to slip into my realm and affect my process. Upon reflection, I realized my progress was being hindered by fear and doubt. Once I became aware of the anchors, I was able to work toward releasing them. Believe me, it took time and work to release the anchors, and still they kept trying to sneak back into my psyche. I had to look in the mirror and do some serious shifting.

How did I overcome the limitations? Positive affirmations, reading books to boost my confidence, stilling the negative self-talk, believing in myself, surrounding myself with loving supportive friends and family, etc. Please remember that we are all learning and growing. And just because you learned one lesson, or released one anchor, doesn't mean that it might not show up in another aspect of your life. This is a journey. So, remember that the laws work if you work them! Now that I've initiated the adjustments and realigned myself with the process, life is manifesting more in line with my expectations.

It all begins to fit together and I am enjoying a world of greater understanding and greater awareness of the world all around. It's all so simple once you are provided the knowledge and view it through new lenses of perception.

Yes, it is prayer and meditation and the application of the Law of Attraction that completes the process and puts our ship on course. It is prayer and meditation that serves as the agent to clean the static off the line and clear the airwaves for crystal-clear communication with Source Energy.

Can you hear me now? Aha! Is this great stuff or what? I love it!

Now all that's left to complete the transformation from victim to victor is to *Reclaim Your Power* and take control of your life's destination.

From Victim to Victor

Transformation from victim to victor represents such an important milestone in the process to take control of your life that it dictates we allot some time to address this matter. In a brief review, we began this voyage analyzing humanity's proclivity toward victimization mentality. Furthermore, we examined the African Americans' heightened proclivity in the direction of a victimization mentality brought on and enhanced through the system of white supremacy. We discussed how a victim mentality manifests as we relinquish the control of our lives to the dictates of others. Allowing others to tell us how to act, think, and behave creates a system of "Boxes" that encloses us and restricts our very being. Afraid of repercussions, we remain contained within the boxes and ultimately become victims of the systems. We become mental and spiritual slaves afraid to push the issue and ask the questions, so we conform.

Furthermore, we discussed how the advent of white supremacy served to intensify the tendency toward victim mentally for the African American. The addition of extreme violence and oppression created seemingly stronger, bigger, and more numerous boxes to imprison the African American consciousness, resulting in a deeper reluctance to buck the system or step out of the box.

During the course of our journey, we've acquired the knowledge and the tools to break out of the boxes. We chiseled holes in the walls so we could see some light. We unscrewed the hinges and took hammers to knock down the walls. We now possess the tools and techniques required to bust out of those super-duper, steel-laden boxes.

It's time to regain control of our lives and regain control of our destinies; it's time to reclaim our power. Completing the transformation from victim to victor requires we enact two of the Keys to Resurrection previously covered: *Responsibility* and *Release*.

Becoming a victor in control of your mind, body, and soul requires you take responsibility for your life, with no more blaming anyone for anything. In addition, it requires you to release the anchors of limitation, let go of all the limiting beliefs, and bust out of the boxes. In order to transform from victim to victor, we must BELIEVE we have the power! It is a matter of incorporating all of the knowledge you've acquired thus far. We must believe in the Universal Laws. Know that they are exact; know that they work every day and every time. We must practice prayer and meditation in conjunction with the Law of Attraction.

Next, take the responsibility and change your life. Taking this step requires that you relinquish the *belief* that someone else is responsible for what shows up in your life. In other words, relinquish the victim mentality of blaming others for your situation, or believing that others have control over you.

Subsequently, you cannot change your situation if you believe you have no control. It renders you subservient; you begin to feel less worthy, not deserving of better, or steeped in self-pity. Feeling sorry for yourself and that the world or others are against you, you become sad or depressed. If you do not take responsibility, then you will be controlled or forever remain a victim.

> *If it's never our fault, we can't take responsibility for it. If we can't take responsibility for it, we'll always be its victim.*
> **– Richard Bach**
>
> *Self-pity is easily the most destructive of the non-pharmaceutical narcotics; it is addictive; gives momentary pleasure; and separates the victim from reality.* **– John W. Gardner**

As previously stated, the victim mentality is prevalent in the human condition. And let's face it, there are no shortages of less-than-desirable conditions since we humans find ourselves in poverty, abusive relationships, disabilities, religious oppression, gender biases, and all of the "-isms" such as racism, sexism, and ageism. I could go on and on.

However, it is my belief that the prevalence of the victim mentality in humanity is caused through socialization. The social institutions teach us to search externally for the answers, from our teachers, leaders, etc. They prompt us to look externally for someone to save us—be it our government, our religious leaders, or our external savior—and to believe that someone else has the responsibility and thus, the control over our lives.

No wonder we have become a nation and a world steeped in a victim mentality. Functioning from the perception of a victim affects your self-esteem, ambitions, achievements, successes, etc. You cannot perform to the best of your abilities with a victim mentality.

Are you a victim or a victor? Are you empowered and in control, or have you surrendered your power to others?

Reversing the victim mentality is a process. It begins with recognizing the condition to be validated and assessing where it is present in your life. Then it requires changing your belief system and taking action to change your realities.

Gratitude and Forgiveness

Two qualities that assist tremendously in reversing the victim mentality are gratitude and forgiveness. When thoughts of victimization creep into your head, such as the *poor-me* syndrome, change your mindset to thoughts of gratitude. Write a list of things you are grateful for. Or think of a situation in which someone in the world has it worse off than you. You will be amazed at how empowering these activities can be. It will help you shift your thinking.

Forgiveness is also very powerful in reversing the *victim* mentality—or, shall I say, in claiming your *victor* mentality.

One of the best reasons to forgive can be found in this quote by Catherine Ponder:

When you hold resentment toward another, you are bound to that person or condition by an emotional link that is stronger than steel. Forgiveness is the only way to dissolve that link and get free.

Humanity is in the midst of evolutionary times. We are entering the Age of Aquarius, an era of enlightenment, a Golden Age. We are entering the 12,000-year ascension portion of a new 26,000-year Earth cycle. Humanity is destined to ascend. Humanity is destined to raise its consciousness.

In order to rise, we must relinquish the victim mentality. It requires that we change our thinking and our behavior. It requires that we utilize the Universal Laws and that we enact the powers we already possess.

Armed with the understanding of prayer and meditation in conjunction with the Universal Laws, you now know You Have the Power! The choice is yours as to what you do with the information. The time is now. *Reclaim Your Power.*

CATCH THE WAVE – *Chapter Summary*

IMPORTANT POINTS TO REMEMBER

- Prayer…is talking to God and asking for what you want.
- Meditation…is listening to God and quieting the mind so you can hear the answers.
- You were created in the image of God; you, too, have the powers of creation and manifestation.
- Prayer and Meditation set the Law of Attraction into action.
- The Law of Attraction works…if you work it!
- You create your own reality.

ACTION STEPS
- If you feel like you're begging when you pray…STOP IT!
- Learn to pray with focus and purpose.
- Learn to meditate and incorporate the practice into your daily routine.
- Take responsibility for your life. Release the victim mentality and become the victor.
- Create a list of goals. Now take yourself through the process of the Law of Attraction and manifest your goals into reality.
- Remember…you have the Power Within!

LIFE LESSONS FOR TRANSFORMATION

AND YOU SAY GOD IS Who, What, And Where?

Just to be clear for the purposes of this section, my reference to God is synonymous with the Supreme Being, the Prime Creator, God Source Energy, the All, the One.

What is your concept of God? Do any of these perceptions give you pause, or cause to wonder?

God is within, thus I AM God.

God is in heaven, and I must seek externally to access HIM/HER.

God is within, thus, I AM God, but I must ask for help from the ancestors, spirits, angels, Ascended Masters, etc.

God is within, but God is also out in the heavens, so I can't be God.

I have the powers of creation; I can manifest that which I desire. I am, in fact, a co-creator of the universe with God. So does this make me God too, or not.

Well, which one is it?!

Confused?! I know I was for quite some time. For a while it seemed that the more I learned and received answers to my questions, the questions changed and I needed more answers. Grappling with some of the metaphysical views, such as "God is within," and "I, too, am God" was a journey for me and quite difficult at times. Finally, I've settled on a concept of God that makes sense to me, at least for today. Certainly this is a very subjective and personal matter. Please allow me to share my thoughts on the subject. Then exercise your due diligence and come to rest with the concept of God that feels compatible with your heart.

Submersed in the concepts of Western philosophy, for most of my young life I perceived God as an amorphous being, existing somewhere in the heavens—that is to say a God with human characteristics, existing externally and totally outside, or removed from my being. With continued study of Eastern philosophy and metaphysics, my perception of God changed remarkably.

Incorporating the metaphysical concepts of Universal Law within my paradigm afforded me the possibility to conceive the oneness of God. So, if there is only the ONE, and everything is connected, then am I not the ONE also? Or, at least part of the ONE?

Furthermore, if I was created in the image of God and I, too, have the powers of creation/manifestation, doesn't that mean that I, too, am God? Or that I am at least a co-creator of the universe with God? It all made sense, but it still just didn't feel right—me claiming to be God. Or even a part of God.

I ebbed and flowed back and forth between being comfortable saying any one of combinations of the following: God is within me; I am co-creator of the universe; I am a part of God; I AM God.

If all of this wasn't confusing enough, I had yet another question that really bugged me for a while. If I have everything I need inside of me and if I am God (or any of the aforementioned aspects), then why do I have to ask for help from my ancestors, guardian angels, spirit guides, the Orisha, the Ascended Masters (Jesus, Buddha, Muhammad, etc.)? Isn't that looking for help externally?

The answer lies in the comment I made earlier explaining that we live in all the dimensions simultaneously. Well, *YOU* are **ALL** of the above. You *are* your ancestors; you *are* the angels; you *are* Jesus, Buddha, Muhammad; and, yes, you *are* God. Oh boy, have I gone and done it now!

Okay, I'm going to give it my best shot to explain, so batten down the hatches, grab hold to something, and let's do this!

Just as the energy of the One has spread to universal proportions, the essence that is you is spread over a vast area. As we descend in consciousness, or become less aware that we are connected to the One, we believe that we are separate from the ONE. Thus, the more separate we perceive ourselves to be, the less we are aware or conscious of our power. In a state of disconnectedness, we have forgotten who we are; thus, we cannot or do not access the full potential of the Supreme Being.

Our ultimate journey is to raise our consciousness and awareness, remember who we are, join all of our higher selves, and consciously reconnect to the ONE. Please note that when I say "reconnect," I really mean "remember," because we already are connected…we have simply forgotten. Since there is only the One, and all and everything is connected, separation is but another part of the illusion.

So what does it mean to "reconnect?" This means taking the journey.

In order to reconnect, we must take the steps, learn the lessons, and raise our vibration. Earth is but a school for our souls. We are in the Third Dimension, very much akin to being in the third grade. In order for us to join those in higher dimensions (or grades), we must do the work, learn how to act, and learn the lessons. We certainly would not allow a third-grader to hang out on the university campus.

Well, until we learn our lessons and learn how to behave and conduct ourselves in accordance to Universal Law, we are not allowed to visit the higher grade levels (dimensions), or roam around the universe.

I remember someone told me that all the water on the planet is the same water that has been here since the beginning of time—every drop. I don't know if that is true, but what a concept! Similarly, I believe that energy never dies; it just changes. That would denote that all of the energy that exists now is the same energy that existed *in the beginning*! This means that when the ONE decided to multiply, all that exists now is the result…including you! Hmmm…life lessons for transformation.

Well, there you have it; that was my best shot. I certainly hope it provided some answers, or at least material for introspection. Each of us is on our own journey. And each of you will relate to this information in the manner that best suits you. Let your heart be your guide.

**RISE to Your Greatest Potential
RAISE the Collective Consciousness**

Epilogue

The Resurrection

UP, UP, You Mighty Race!!

So, my fellow Navigators, we have arrived at our destination and the time has come to say, "So Long." Thank you for your courage to explore these new horizons and set sail across a sea of uncertainty, allowing me to share my journey. Consequently, I've shared my "aha" moments and a bit of my soul. It is my sincerest intention that my journey and this information have been of value along your path to take control of your life and Navigate Your Existence.

Life is a journey full of various destinations; this has been just one of many. In the event you didn't know it before, the ultimate journey (or final destination) is to consciously reconnect to the ONE (Source Energy, God). I say "consciously" because you already are connected to the ONE—as has always been the case, just merely forgotten.

But worry not, for you are living in a great time period, a time of the great awakening. The energy and resurgence of the knowledge we need to awaken is forthcoming in a myriad of scenarios all around us.

As we surge ahead experiencing change in this great time of transition, humanity will be forced to continuously look back and examine the significance of December 21, 2012.

The world will be forced to reconcile with the magnitude and the tremendous implications of the simultaneous ending of numerous world cycles and the beginning of the same. The effects of 2012 are not over; they are just beginning and will be upon us for the next 26,000 years. How you fare throughout this transition is up to you. Some will put 2012 behind them as if it was just another year gone by; others will continue to analyze it in order to make sense of the events as they continue to unfold.

With increased comprehension of energy, comes increased awareness that we are all connected, whether we know it or not. Whether we want to accept it or not, all are connected to the heartbeat of the Earth and the Divine flow of the universe. That being said, with guarded anticipation, I yearn for the day when all beings coexist in the balance and harmony of the One. The planet is on the Rise; Humanity is on the Rise; and it is time for us as African Americans to Rise.

My grandmother used to say, "It is always darkest before the dawn." As a people, amidst the progress we've accomplished, sometimes the forecast appears bleak. Penal incarceration rates are astronomical and unemployment rates are as high as ever. While certain segments of the African American community search to discover cultural roots, far too many remain submerged in cultural apathy. That being said, I hold fast the quote by Fredrick Douglass: "Only through struggle comes progress."

Our journey as Africans has been long; our narrative extensive. From the beginning of time till the present, we have experienced the highest of highs (i.e., The Golden Age of Africa) to the lowest of lows (slavery). Like all journeys, we must travel the high tide along with the low tide. It is all part of the earthly experience, inasmuch as it is a part of the cosmic cycles of the universe.

It is my contention that we as a people are experiencing the end of a major cycle and on the brink of a new grand design. It's time to catch the wave.

It's time for the Resurrection of the African-American spirit—the African spirit. Yes, you who built the Pyramids 5,000 to 10,000 years ago…that still stand.

It's time for a great Resurrection of the African-American people:

A Resurrection from the Dead—a death induced by lack of knowledge…the loss of Knowledge of Self.

A Resurrection from the Project mentality, the Victim mentality, the Second-Class mentality, and the Assimilation mentality.

Armed with the knowledge within these pages, TRUTH is at hand.

Endowed with TRUTH, claim your personal power on a third-dimensional level.

Inspired by TRUTH, claim, your spiritual power on a fifth-dimensional level.

It's time to BREAK OUT OF THE BOX, bust through the walls, and release those anchors of limitation. Change your mind and change your reality. Don't have a job? Create one! Stop waiting for someone to give you anything. You have everything you need! Turn off that TV and reclaim your mind. Read a book; learn a skill. Learn and reclaim who you are—the greatness that once was ours.

As African-Americans we must come to terms with a stark reality: we live in a European-dominated society. No longer operating within the confines of our cultural systems, it is no longer our "house." Accordingly, we must stop believing that if we just look, act, and think like Europeans (or assimilate into their culture), we can move into their house (assimilate into their system) and expect them to share the goodies or give us anything.

Dr. Boyce Watkins speaks to this issue best in an article entitled, "Why Black People Don't Get Hired: The Dr. Boyce Explanation." (See www.yourblackworld.net.) He states:

Would you let someone move into your house and then shift around the furniture? No, you would not. After all, it's your house, you built it, and you make the rules. The only way you might even consider allowing someone to stay in your house (which you probably would not) is if they do what you say and live by your rules. Moving the furniture is probably not even an option, and if it is, they can only move things after getting your approval.

....If you truly want to be free, get off the psychological and economic plantation and take pride in creating your own business...Stop letting the world set your limitations...

....The only way to get power and true equality is to learn to build and develop something yourself and not wait for someone else to save you.

...True freedom, equality and opportunity are created, not given. Self-sufficiency is the ultimate cure for racism.

Thank you, Dr. Watkins.

True liberation is about embracing and owning our higher mystical roots as souls and as part of a magnificent cultural and spiritual heritage. It's about reconnecting with our innate wisdom and the spiritual freedom, tapping the compass within for true self-empowerment.

It is said that confused people do nothing. If you are waiting for someone to do anything for you, you have relinquished your power and become a victim. There is no need to be a victim; it's time to step into your greatness.

Now that we have been exposed to the wonders of melanin, we recognize the remarkable potential for transformation. The phenomenon that is melanin has the potential to transcend beyond transformation and move on to the Resurrection of the African American population.

Resurrection means *to rise from the dead*. Yes, we as African Americans have suffered a mental, spiritual, and even physical death, and we have yet to recover. I believe that in the coming years, the discussion of melanin will be on the tips of many a tongue. And I believe that, as we understand melanin and attribute it to what makes us Black, it will trigger a renaissance of the '60s when James Brown made it cool to be Black… "I'm Black and I'm proud." This renaissance will spur a desire to know more about who we are now and who we once were.

Yes, I believe the melanin phenomenon will provide that spark to ignite the Resurrection of the African American spirit. Still, there is a premium benefit that we have yet to discuss: the remarkable potential for resurrection of Black people all over the world, all across the African diaspora.

The Knowledge is At Hand;
The Onus is Upon You;
Break Out of the Box and
Your Resurrection,
   Your True Liberation,
      Your Power are All Yours to Claim!

Complete the transformation from victim to victor. Be a victor; live victoriously. Do the work: read, study, practice, and teach. Take responsibility for your life. Be the conductor of your ship and Navigate Your Existence!

You, who built the Pyramids…you have everything you need. It is buried deep inside; enclosed in your genetic memory. The time is now to *Reclaim Your Power*. The time is now for that great Resurrection of the African American Mind, Body, and Soul.

It's time to:

    Step up

        Stand up

            Wake up

                and Catch the Wave!

Seize this great wave of cosmic energy that is upon us because it's STAR time. It is time to begin a new cycle, one of completion—from the Pyramids to the Projects, and from the Projects to the Stars!!

Up, Up, You Mighty Race,
You Can Accomplish What You Will!
– The Honorable Marcus Garvey

7 Keys to the African American Resurrection

Revisited

Our journey to the stars commences with the 7 Keys to the African American Resurrection. Each Key unlocks the secrets to the ensuing Resurrection of the African American Mind, Body, and Soul emancipating your spirit.

RECOGNIZE – The Anchors of Limitation

We must recognize what's holding us back and weighing us down. Identify the anchors. Only by identifying the problem can one begin the path to the solution. Now it's time for some deep self-reflection; it's time to write *your story*. Time to identify the anchors, or the limiting beliefs, in *your* personal and spiritual life. Then let the healing, the transformation, the resurrection begin.

Your Story

Identify Anchors ("-isms," systems of belief)

Identify your Anchor(s) of Limitation

RESTORE – The Knowledge of the Ancestors

"As Above; So Below." There is nothing new under the sun. Return to the knowledge of the ancestors. You who built the pyramids—the essence of that spirit resides in you. It is a matter of waking up the sleeping giant, the memory of your past; it is all encoded in your genetic memory. *Restore the Knowledge of the Ancestors.*

Time Waits For No One

Everything is Connected
Now You See It - Now You Don't
New Age/Ancient Wisdom

☥ RESPONSIBILITY – Take Responsibility

☥ RELEASE –The Anchors

You create your own reality. *Take Responsibility* for what shows up in your life—the good, the bad, and the ugly. If you don't like the picture, then change it. Release the baggage of the past. No more excuses; no more blaming others. You cannot complete the transformation from victim to victor until you *Release the Anchors* and claim full responsibility for your existence.

Karma/Reincarnation

☥ REACTIVATE Your Energy Sources

We must reactivate and energize our internal power sources connecting our internal and external energies to the One Source. Consciously connecting is the key! Just like a car requires service, so, too, does the vessel that is YOU! Inspect, clean, fuel, and activate your energy sources habitually. Maintain your energy sources in optimal condition for peak performance.

Melanin, Energy, and You
Ignite the Internal Flames

☥ RECLAIM Your Power

To *Reclaim Your Power*, go within. You already possess everything you need. Develop a discipline of prayer and meditation in conjunction with the Law of Attraction and create your new reality. Manifest the personal and spiritual life you desire and deserve.

Prayer, Meditation, and the Law of Attraction

☥ RISE to Your Greatest Potential and RAISE the Collective Consciousness

RISE to Your Greatest Potential

Embrace the 7 KEYS and allow the secrets of empowerment to unfold. Incorporate these steps into your life and make the shift from victim to victor. Be the conductor of your own reality; chart your own course. Transform your personal and spiritual life, and *Rise*. As you *Rise,* so too will your vibration, your soul, and your spirit. So *Rise to Your Greatest Potential...* which is Infinite and Limitless!

RAISE the Collective Consciousness

It is your duty to rise. It is your personal and spiritual duty to rise as we seek our final destination— reconnection with Source Energy, the ONE. As you rise and raise your vibration, you in turn affect your environment. Good vibes are contagious.

For each of you who rise and raise your vibration, you raise your consciousness. As you Raise your consciousness, you, in turn:

    Raise the consciousness of our African American family,
    Raise the consciousness of humanity,
    Raise the consciousness of the planet,
    And RAISE the Collective Consciousness.

THE WORLD IS IN DIVINE ORDER

Everything is connected; we are all connected. We share the same mind, as part of the great universal mind, the collective consciousness of the ONE. And all of humanity is connected to the heartbeat of the Earth. As humanity comes into balance and harmony, so too will our planet.

As each of you RISE, reach back and RAISE another. Am I my brother's keeper? Yes, I am.

The world is in Divine order. There is no such thing as an accident. It is not an accident that you are reading this book. Every soul on this planet is traveling on his or her own journey. We are all spiritual light beings on a journey back to the One, back to consciously reconnecting to the One. Each of us chose this experience; we chose our bodies, our parents, and our lessons to learn for this earthly trip. So all people—each soul—is exactly who they should be for this earthly sojourn. How you choose to Navigate Your Existence is totally up to you.

Thus, my fellow Navigators,

Now you know the secret to freedom; you hold the 7 Keys to Resurrection.

Now it's up to you to be the conductor of your ship. You must take the helm and control the rudder. Continue to search and research. Focus on discipline and stay committed to practice as you continue your journey.

The more you stay on course, the steadier the trip. The steadier the course, the more the ship will increase in velocity. As the velocity increases, soon you will no longer need a ship. The essence which is you—the energy—*becomes* the vessel as you blast off into hyper drive. Now, ignite the power within and Navigate Your Existence!

YOU HAVE EVERYTHING YOU NEED TO
NAVIGATE YOUR EXISTENCE!
BON VOYAGE!

Appendix

Bibliography

Africa, Llaila, *MELANIN What Makes Black People Black!,* Seaburn Publishing Group, Long Island City, New York 2009

Afua, Queen, *HEAL THYSELF for Health and Longevity,* A & B Publishers Group, Brooklyn, NY 2002

Barnes, Carol, *MELANIN: THE CHEMICAL KEY TO BLACK GREATNESS,* Melanin Technologies, Houston, TX 1988

Barton, Paul Alfred, *A History of the African-Olmecs: Black Civilizations of America from Prehistoric Times to the Present Era,* Authorhouse, 2001

Browder, Anthony T., *Nile Valley Contributions to Civilization-Exploding the Myths, Volume 1,* The Institute of Karmic Guidance, Washington, D.C. 1992

Drunvalo, Melchizedek, *THE ANCIENT SECRET OF THE FLOWER OF LIFE, Volume 1,* Light Technology Publishing, Flagstaff, AZ 1990

Emoto, Masaru, *THE HIDDEN MESSAGES IN WATER,* Beyond Words Publishing, Inc., Hillsboro, Oregon 2004

Joseph, Frank, *The Lost Civilization of Lemuria: The Rise and Fall of the World's Oldest Culture,* Inner Traditions/Bear & Company, 2006

Khamit-Kush, Indus, *What They Never Told You in History Class,* A & B Publishers Group, Brooklyn, NY 1983

Latif, Sultan and Latif, Naimah, *SLAVERY: The African American PSYCHIC TRAUMA,* Latif Communications Group, Inc., Chicago, IL 1994

Milanovich, Norma and McCune, Shirley, *The Light Shall Set You Free,* Athena Publishing, Scottsdale, AZ 2005

Moore, T. Owens, *Dark Matters Dark Secrets,* Zamami Press, Redan, GA 2002

Rogers, J.A., *100 AMAZING FACTS ABOUT THE NEGRO With Complete Proof,* Helga M. Rogers, St Petersburg, FL 1995

Russell, Kathy, and Wilson, Midge, and Hall, Ronald, *The Color Complex – The Politics of Skin Color Among African Americans,* Harcourt Brace Jovanovich, Publishers, New York 1992

Van Sertima, Ivan, *They Came Before Columbus: The African Presence in Ancient America,* Random House Publishing Group, New York 1976

Vanzant, Iyanla, *Tapping the Power Within – A Path to Self-Empowerment for Black Women,* Harlem River Press, New York London 1992

Weatherford, Jack, *Indian Givers: How Native Americans Transformed the World,* Crown Publishing Group 2010

Welsing, Frances Cress, *THE ISIS PAPERS-The Keys To The Colors,* Third World Press, Chicago, IL 1991

Woodson, Carter G., *The Mis-Education of the Negro,* African World Press, Trenton, NJ 1993

A Note from the Author

In Search of Self – The Resurrection of Our Name

"What should we call you??" Have you ever been asked that question? I have...and I now reflect on how many times my answer has changed over the years.

For some time I have had this discussion with myself in an effort to ascertain the true and accurate name of my people. Who are we? Who am I? Is it even necessary to have a name, a nationality? Technically, I say *no*. After all, aren't all humans inhabitants of the planet, citizens of the universe? However, when dealing with our third dimensional realm—our earthly political, social, and economical systems in which we function—it becomes necessary at some level to identify oneself in terms of nationality, and/or race. In addition, as we recognize that groups of humans do possess varying characteristics, it becomes necessary to utilize names/terms for clarification. Humans have been on this planet for a very long time, and the names used for identification by self or by others have also changed numerous times.

That being said, let me begin with the names I've been called, or that I've called myself:

Negro – A term assigned to us as slaves in 1779

Colored – A term assigned to us as slaves in 1779

Black – In an effort to distance ourselves from the terms *Negro* and *Colored,* in the '60s, we proudly proclaimed *I'm Black and I'm Proud.*

Black (or dark) has been used to describe us as a people through the ages, mostly through various associations. We must appreciate its association with the country of Kemet/Egypt (Khem means black) along with so many of the names of the "African" countries: Somalia/Black; Sudan/Black

Khem is also the stem of *khemistry/chemistry*—a term used to describe the study of matter (dark matter….or black). Which brings us to the topic of melanin (dark matter)—a black molecule—*The Khemical/Chemical Key to Life.*

Although black is used to denote us as a race, it is really an adjective, not a noun—which would be the correct part of speech for a proper "name"—and though it has been used to describe a people, it is not a "name" or "nationality."

Afro-American – In an effort to further identify ourselves, we took on the description of Afro-American. *Afro* is not the name of a nation or a continent, thus, it does not suffice as an accurate descriptor as a nationality.

African – (see below)

African American - Although I do use the term, I have some difficulty with **African** American for several reasons: One, Africa is a continent, not a nation. Therefore, it does not suffice as a nationality. Secondly, the continent was assigned the name "Africa" by the Greeks, after a Roman General named **Publius Cornelius Scipio Africanus** (236–183 BC). So, technically the term *African American* is a continuation of Roman colonialization. Although the land commonly known as Africa was known as several terms, **Alkebulan** and **Amexem**, are both recognized as ancient indigenous names for Africa.

At this point I would imagine one would agree there is certainly a need to continue the discussion—the search as to *who* we are.

There is quite a bit of research required to correct years of misinformation that has been inducted into His-story books and "ladened" upon the minds of humanity. As we come into the Age of Aquarius/the age of enlightenment when truth shall rise once more and as we transition through the "end times" when everything upside down will be set right-side up, it is essential that we continue to search for truth. As evidenced from our past, we can continue to allow others to define us (name us) or we can select that by which we choose to be defined. What should I call you? Ultimately, it is *you* who must decide how you want to be identified. This speaks to the Kwanzaa principle Kujichagulia—Self Determination—to define ourselves, name ourselves, create for ourselves, and speak for ourselves. I say it is imperative to exercise your due diligence and actively search for the *Truth*. The saga continues to restore us to the Greatness that once was Ours.

In search of self, the resurrection continues as we strive to reclaim our true identity. In your quest, please allow me to suggest some important topics of study and several resources:

The History of Moorish Americans
The Olmecs
Atlantis
The Ancient Moors from Lemuria - *The Moors(Mu or MUU or Muur or Muir or Moor) from Lemuria* (El'MUUria – Le'Muria – LeMUURia)

Resources:

Van Sertima, Ivan, *They Came Before Columbus: The African Presence in Ancient America,* Random House Publishing Group, New, York, 1976

Weatherford, Jack, *Indian Givers: How Native Americans Transformed the World,* Crown Publishing group, 2010

Barton, Paul Alfred, *A History of the African-Olmecs: Black Civilizations of America from Prehistoric Times to the Present Era,* Authorhouse, 2001

Joseph, Frank, *The Lost Civilization of Lemuria: The Rise and Fall of the World's Oldest Culture,* Inner Traditions/Bear & Company, 2006

The Journey Continues!!

About the Author

OMIYALE JUBÉ IS THE **CEO** AND FOUNDER OF *NAVIGATE YOUR Existence,* an organization designed to open new portals of understanding for those who desire to **"Take Control of their Life's Destination."**

Omiyale, was born and raised on 125th street in Harlem, New York. Early in life, at the whim of the New York City school system, she was labeled culturally deprived, underprivileged, and emotionally disturbed. She is a survivor of abusive relationships and an attempted suicide. Her journey began searching for answers. Omiyale's discovery of her rich African heritage restored a sense of being, a step towards claiming self-worth. Yet, still looking externally for answers and not feeling in control, the quest continued. Searching for answers on a spiritual level opened doors to understanding her being on a more profound level, her very existence.

Omiyale's journey consisted of a series of *"aha"* moments that *simplified* the most complex and sometimes misunderstood concepts of life, converting them to tools of empowerment fueling her transformation.

She possesses an uncanny ability to provide answers to those yet unanswered, nagging questions about life, provide new perspectives with which to view the world, and guide individuals to look within for direction.

Sharing these *"aha"* moments affords her an extraordinary connection to her audiences as she guides them to ignite the power within. She utilizes her journey to teach others how to find their internal compass, and chart their course of destination. Omiyale's journey as an acclaimed speaker and commitment to service has won her numerous awards and recognition from various organizations and persons of distinction.

Currently, Omiyale resides in Las Vegas, Nevada. Amongst her accomplishes, she is an Author, Inspirational Speaker, Personal and Spiritual Coach, and Reiki Master. A retired school administrator, she has always been inspired to share knowledge, effect change, and champion the evolution of humanity. Her speaking and coaching series is dedicated to the resurrection of mind, body, and soul, and to the ascension of consciousness for the human collective.

Navigate Your Existence!
The Foundation

Navigate Your Existence is a foundation designed to open new portals of understanding for those who desire to Take Control of their Life's Destination. Taking the "mystique" out of metaphysics provides the information everyone needs to ignite their internal energies and rise to their peak potential on the journey to self-empowerment, self-actualization, and personal transformation. *Navigate Your Existence* affords you the knowledge, tools, and techniques required to take control of your personal and spiritual life, so you may enjoy physical, personal, and spiritual success. The *Navigate Your Existence* speaking and coaching series is dedicated to the resurrection of mind, body, and soul, and to the ascension of consciousness for the human collective.

Join us!

Navigate Your Existence
Omiyale Jubé CEO and Founder
www.NavigateYourExistence.com

Omiyale Jubé

Inspirational Speaker, Workshop Trainer, Personal and Spiritual Life Coach

Are you Ready??

Are you ready to Take Control of Your Life's Destination?

Omiyale provides the Knowledge, Tools, and Techniques required to: Release the Anchors of Limitation And Rise to Your Greatness Potential!

The **Navigate Your Existence** speaking and seminar series is dedicated to the ascension of humanity through the resurrection of Mind, Body, and Soul.

Take the Journey!

Hire Omiyale for your next event:

Omiyale is available for
KEYNOTE
SEMINARS
WORKSHOP TRAINING
GUEST SPEAKER
COACHING

Contact:
Booking @NavigateYourExistence.com
www.NavigateYourExistence.com

"Omiyale Jubé is the consummate navigator, guiding the uninitiated and even those with some familiarity, through the paths of universal wisdom and ENERGY. If you have questions about the highways of the Universe and your route on them, Omiyale has the metaphysical and cultural maps that reveal the way. An invigorating speaker, Omiyale holds her audiences captivated with her library of information."

– Leah Young, Founder the iMASTERY(TM) Institute.